GOOGLE

USER GUIDE

MW00887215

The Complete Step By Step Practical Guide To Learn How To Master The New Google Pixel 8a For Beginners & Seniors. With Step-By-Step Instructions And Android Tips & Tricks

By

Matt E. Walker

Table of Contents

INTRODUCTION

Google Pixels are renowned for their exceptional photography skills, and the new Pixel 8a is no exception. Google describes the handset's 64MP, 13MP dual-camera system as 'AI-mazing', and it comes preloaded with a slew of wonderful AI capabilities that make edits like magic.

The 'Best Take' feature corrects any face defects, such as blinking or yawning, and replaces them with your preferred snap, resulting in consistently stunning group photos. Furthermore, Audio Magic Eraser, which is now only accessible on Google's 8 series devices, successfully removes annoying background noise in films, such as wind or motor revving sounds. Finally, the Magic Editor lets you change photo backdrops, reposition things, and even make them disappear using the Magic Eraser tool. All of these capabilities combined make the Google Pixel 8a camera a formidable power.

The Google Pixel 8a's Pixel Call Assist capabilities offer a seamless calling experience from start to finish. An increased background noise filter lets you hear your caller even in noisy situations, making it great for those 'where are you' phone calls at a concert or in a bar.

Alternatively, the 'Hold for Me' option will wait on hold for you, whether you're in a doctor's queue or somewhere else, and notify you when your turn comes up next. Furthermore, the Google Pixel 8a's powerful spam filter handles the vexing problem of spam calls. You can now get only the calls you desire, which is a big gain for Google.

The days of having your phone die unexpectedly in the middle of the day are over. The Google Pixel 8a's battery lasts more than 24 hours (72 hours with Extreme Battery Saver activated). Now you can make the most of your Pixel for longer than ever!

Google launched the 'Circle to Search' function in 2024, allowing Android users a new and faster way to search without switching apps. Users may rapidly Google anything they wish to learn more about by simply a simple circular gesture. For example, you may instantly look up the brand of a purse in an Instagram photo or identify a celebrity's face. As one may imagine, this revolutionary feature is accessible on the Pixel 8a!

FEATURES OF GOOGLE PIXEL 8A

Specifications

SoC	Google Tensor G3
Display type	OLED, 120Hz
Display dimensions	6.1-inch
Display resolution	1080 x 2400
RAM	8GB
Storage	128GB, 256GB
Battery	4,492mAh
Charge speed	18W wired, 7.5W wireless
Charge options	Wired, Wireless
Ports	USB-C
SIM support	Nano SIM, eSIM
Operating System	Android 14
Front camera	13MP, f/2.2
Rear camera	64MP, f/1.89, OIS main; 13MP, f/2.2 ultrawide
Cellular connectivity	4G, 5G (optional mmWave)
Wi-Fi connectivity	Wi-Fi 6E
Bluetooth	Bluetooth 5.3
Dimensions	152.1 x 72.7 x 8.9mm
Weight	188g
IP Rating	IP67
Colors	Obsidian, Porcelain, Bay, Aloe
Price	$499

Design

The 8a, like its flagship sibling, has a camera bar that runs across the back of the phone, giving Google handsets their distinct appearance.

However, the Pixel 8a features more rounded sides than the rest of the Pixel 8 range. The Pixel 8a also has a matte back and an aluminum frame, as well as a larger bezel at the bottom of the display than one would anticipate from a premium gadget.

The Pixel 8a is IP67 water resistant, which means you can immerse it in up to 3 feet of water without danger. The phone contains more recycled materials than previous models, with aluminum, glass, and plastic all derived from previously used components.

Color possibilities include obsidian, porcelain, bay, and aloe, or black, white, blue, and green if you want to omit the marketing words. These are essentially the same colors that Google offers for the Pixel 8 Pro.

Display

The Pixel 8a's screen appears to be identical to the Pixel 7a's. It features a 6.1-inch panel, which is slightly smaller than the Pixel 8's 6.2-inch display. However, the Pixel 8a has more in common with the Pixel 8 than you may assume in terms of screen, as the midrange phone now features the Actua display that Google uses on its flagship phones.

In terms of practical benefits, the Pixel 8a has a maximum brightness of 2,000 nits, which is the same as the Pixel 8 rating. The Pixel 7a, on the other hand, reached 1,000 nits, indicating that the next model's screen will be much brighter.

The Pixel 8a also offers a higher refresh rate, which may increase to 120Hz when on-screen activity necessitates it. This is comparable to Google's flagships and represents a big improvement over the Pixel 7a's 90Hz refresh rate.

Camera

Given that Pixels routinely appear in our top camera phone rankings, Google phones' cameras always get a lot of attention. The Pixel 8a is likely to outperform the 7a in this area, but there are a few notable modifications to the camera technology.

The Pixel 8a keeps the Pixel 7a's 64MP main camera sensor and the 13MP ultrawide camera.

Because of the Tensor G3 chipset (more on that in a moment), the Pixel 8a has the same photo-editing capabilities as the Pixel 8. This includes Best Take, which allows you to switch out different faces in group images to guarantee that everyone is looking at the camera, and Magic Editor, which allows you to easily resize and enhance photos. Audio Magic Eraser can also help you improve the sound quality of your video clip.

Tensor Processor and AI Features.

As previously noted, the Pixel 8a is powered by Google's Tensor G3 system-on-chip, which is also used in the Pixel 8 series. That could result in improved performance since the Tensor G3 outperforms the earlier Tensor G2 found in the Pixel 7 range.

The Tensor G3 chipset's main feature is how Google Phone employs its Tensor engine to enable a wide range of AI capabilities. In addition to the photo editing features stated above, the Pixel 8a supports live translation, which allows you to have discussions with someone who speaks another language that is translated in real-time. Improved Call Assist capabilities are also available, and Circle to Search on the Pixel 8a allows you to quickly look anything up without leaving the current app.

AI features will be a key selling point for the Pixel 8a, not only because they are now popular in the smartphone world, but also because Google's midrange phone is substantially less expensive than Samsung's flagships.

Battery life and charging

The battery capacity has grown since the Pixel 7a, with the Pixel 8a packing a 4,404 mAh cell.

The Pixel 8a, like its predecessor, charges at 18W, and wireless charging remains an option.

Software

Aside from AI technologies, the Pixel 8a's most significant increase over its predecessor may be the level of support Google gives for the phone. The Pixel 8a, along with the Pixel 8 and Pixel 8 Pro, will receive software and security upgrades for seven years.

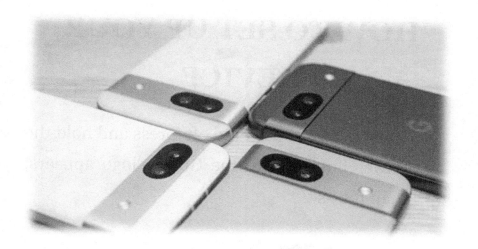

HOW TO SET UP YOUR DEVICE

- If the device is powered off, press and hold the Power button until the Google logo appears, then release.

- From the 'Welcome to your Pixel' screen, choose a language and then tap Get Started.

- Select language.
- From the 'Set up using another device' screen, choose an option.
- Tap Skip to skip this step.
- Set up with another device.
- From the 'Connect to Wi-Fi' screen, select a network and enter the password.

- Once the setup is complete, tap Skip to add a Wi-Fi network.

- If eSIM activation fails over the cellular network, a Wi-Fi network will be required.

- From the 'Phone activation' screen, select Continue.

- If prompted, enter your account PIN and then follow the on-screen directions.

- When activating a new phone, make sure the old one is switched off.

- Choose the desired option from the 'Who are you setting up this phone for' screen, then tap Next.

- For myself.

- For my child.

- On the 'Sign in' screen, enter your Google™ email address and tap Next.

- Once the setup is complete, tap Skip to add your Google account.

On the 'Set a PIN' screen, enter a PIN code and then tap Next.

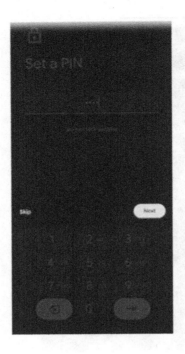

- Tap Screen lock options to customize your pattern or password.

- After the setup process is complete, tap Skip to configure a screen lock, fingerprint recognition, or face recognition.

- From the 'Google services' screen, select the desired options and then tap Accept.

- From the 'Verizon Services' screen, select the desired option and tap I accept.

- To continue, tap I accept on the 'Additional legal terms' screen.

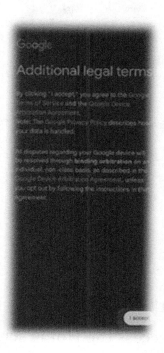

- From the 'Swipe to navigate' screen, select Try it.
- If you don't want to learn gestures for going Home, back, and switching apps, select Skip.

From the 'All set!' screen, swipe up from the bottom of the phone to access the Home screen.

BACK-UP AND STORAGE

How to Back up and restore using a computer.

Learn how to backup and restore your device on a computer.

Transfer media to or from a PC.

Insert the USB-C end of the USB-C cable into the device's bottom port when it is turned on. Connect the USB end of the USB-C cable to an open port on your computer.

To change the device's USB mode, swipe down from the Notification bar and choose Android System > Charging notification > File Transfer / Android Auto or PTP.

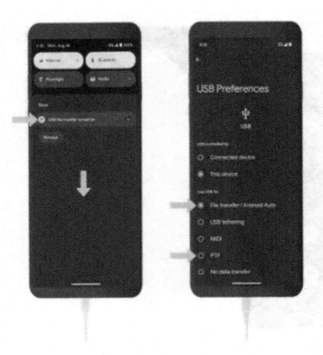

Click the File Explorer icon, then This PC.

Choose the device name and then navigate to the desired folder.

To transfer files, drag and drop them to or from the device's drive.

Transfer Media to or from a Mac:

To communicate between your device and a Mac computer, you must have the Android File Transfer app installed. Download and install the Android File Transfer app.

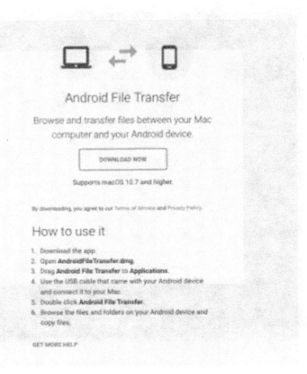

Android File Transfer

Browse and transfer files between your Mac
computer and your Android device.

DOWNLOAD NOW

Supports macOS 10.7 and higher.

By downloading, you agree to our Terms of Service and Privacy Policy.

How to use it

1. Download the app.
2. Open **AndroidFileTransfer.dmg**.
3. Drag **Android File Transfer** to **Applications**.
4. Use the USB cable that came with your Android device and connect it to your Mac.
5. Double click **Android File Transfer**.
6. Browse the files and folders on your Android device and copy files.

GET MORE HELP

With the device powered on, insert the USB-C end of the USB-C cable into the device's port, then connect the USB end to an open port on the computer.

To change the device's USB mode, swipe down from the Notification bar and choose Android System > Charging notification > File Transfer / Android Auto or PTP.

When the phone is connected to the computer, the Android File Transfer software is launched automatically. Choose a folder to transfer files to/from.

Drag and drop the desired files to and from the device you want to transfer.

How to Check Available storage

Check the available device storage, free up memory, uninstall unused apps, and clear app data.

View available memory.

1. Swipe down from the Notification bar with two fingers and select the Settings icon.

2. Select Storage. Available storage will be displayed.

Free up memory.

From the Storage panel, select Free Up Space. Navigate to, select, and hold the required material. Select the "Delete" icon.

Remove unused applications.

From the Settings menu, select Apps > See all apps > and then the desired app. From here, you can uninstall or force-stop the app.

Clear the app data.

From the Settings menu, choose Apps > See all apps > desired app > Storage & cache > Clear storage or cache.

Add storage.

Download a cloud storage app from the Play Store.

How to Backup and Restore with Google.

Learn how to use Google to backup your contacts, photos, and files.

- Swipe down from the notification bar and tap the Settings icon.
- Scroll to and pick Google.

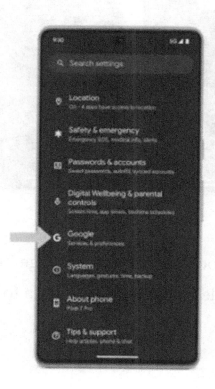

Select Backup. Check that Backup to Google Drive is enabled by selecting the Backup by Google One switch.

If desired, choose Account storage to enable redundancy while backing up your data to the cloud.

Select your preferred backup account choice or click Add account to create a new backup account. When you add your Google account to a device, the previously backed-up data for that Google account is restored.

How to Transfer data from an Android phone to a Pixel.

You can copy data such as texts, photos, music, contacts, calendars, and applications.

To wirelessly transfer data, pair your Android phone with your new Pixel phone.

Tip: To transfer data via USB cable rather than Wi-Fi, tap the image five times on the "Copy apps & data" screen.

Step 1: Prepare both phones for setup.

Important: It is advised that you create a Google account. Otherwise, you will be unable to download apps and certain content will not be transferred to your new Pixel phone.

- To begin, ensure that you have:
- Your fully charged Android phone runs the most recent software.
- Your new Pixel phone is completely charged.
- A dependable Wi-Fi connection.
- If you wish to utilize a real SIM card on your new Pixel, you'll need both the SIM card and an insertion tool.

Step 2: Pair your phones.

- Turn on both your existing Android phone and the new Pixel phone.

43

- On your new Pixel phone, choose Pixel or Android device.
- On your current Android phone, press the Set Up notification. A QR code scanner will appear.
- You can also use your Camera app to manually scan the QR code.
- Scan the QR code on your new Pixel phone with your current Android phone.

Tip: Your current Android phone's active Wi-Fi connection will be transferred to your new Pixel phone. If your Android phone is not already linked to Wi-Fi, connect your Pixel phone to one.

Step 3: Prepare your Pixel phone.

Set up your SIM. If applicable, you can also:

- Download an eSIM from your carrier. To download, simply follow the on-screen directions.

- Transfer your SIM card or eSIM to the Pixel device. To transfer, follow the on-screen instructions.

- Enter the screen lock code from your current Android device into your Pixel phone.

- Your Google Accounts will start to move to your Pixel phone.

- Set up Face and Fingerprint Unlock.

Step 4: Copy the data from the Android device.

If you paired your phone during step two.

Follow the on-screen prompts to choose which data to copy from your current Android handset. You may move data such as apps, Google Accounts, and text messages.

Tip: To transfer data via a USB cable rather than Wi-Fi, press the image five times on the "Copy data from your Android device" screen. You can do this even if you have not yet paired your phones.

- If you did not pair your phone in step 2, hit the "Copy data from your Android device" page five times and then choose Next.
- Turn on and unlock your Android device.
- Connect one end of the Android charging cable to your Android device.
- Connect the other end to the Pixel phone.
- If you have a Quick Switch Adapter, connect it to your Pixel phone.
- If you don't have a charging cable, you can transfer data wirelessly.
- On your Android device, follow the on-screen instructions.
- On your Pixel phone, a data list displays.
- To copy all of your data, choose Copy.
- To duplicate only certain data, disable any superfluous features.
- Tap Copy.
- When the transfer is completed, you can use your phone.

BASIC SETTINGS

How to Charge your Pixel phone

To charge your phone, plug your accessories or other phone on its back.

Your Pixel phone's battery may lose performance over time due to irregular life, temperature and use. Some Pixel phones may automatically alter charging to manage device and battery temperatures, resulting in longer battery life. In rare circumstances, this can lead to reduced charging speed.

Tip: To charge wirelessly, the Battery Share your phone must have a full battery charge. To check your phone's battery level, open the Settings app. Tap Battery, and then Battery Share. Place your phone somewhere that won't get too hot.

How to Charge Your Phone

47

BASIC SETTINGS

How to Charge your Pixel phone

To charge your phone, place your accessories or other phone on its back.

Your Pixel phone's battery may lose performance over time due to usage habits, temperature, and age. Some Pixel phones may automatically alter charging to manage device and battery temperatures, resulting in longer battery life. In rare circumstances, this can lead to reduced charging speeds.

Tip: To charge wirelessly with Battery Share, your phone must have a full battery charge. To check your phone's battery level, open the Settings app. Tap Battery and then Battery Share. Place your phone somewhere that won't get too hot.

How to Charge Your Phone.

- Connect either end of the USB-C cable to the connector on the bottom of your smartphone.

- Connect the opposite end of the cord to the power adapter included with your phone.

- Connect your power adapter to an electrical outlet.

How to Use Adaptive Charging

When you charge your phone for an extended amount of time or overnight, Adaptive Charging may kick in and charge to 100% one hour before you unplug. The Adaptive Charging function extends the battery life.

The Adaptive Charging function learns from your previous charging behavior. Aside from the parameters indicated above, if a lengthy charging session is anticipated, it may still activate.

Tip: The feature takes around 14 days to understand your charging habits. If your charging habits change, such as when you travel, Adaptive Charging may not function.

Turn off adaptive charging:

- Open your phone's Settings app.
- Tap Battery, then Adaptive Charging.
- Turn off Use Adaptive Charging.

Tip: When you enable Adaptive Charging, a notification shows indicating when your battery will be fully charged.

Charging Tips: How to Charge Fast.

Use a wall outlet as a power source. Other power sources, such as laptops, may charge more slowly.

You can use your phone while it is charging. Avoid using it while charging to speed up the charging process.

Hear when your phone is charging.

Make sure your phone's ringtone is turned on.

- Open your phone's Settings app.
- Tap Sound and then Advanced.
- Switch on the charging noises.
- When you plug in your phone, you should hear something.

Note: If your phone is silenced or on vibrate, you will not hear anything.

Show the battery % in the status bar.

- Open your phone's Settings app.
- Tap the battery.
- Turn on the battery percentage.

Check battery life and use.

- Launch your phone's Settings app.
- Under Battery, check how much charge you have left and how long it will last.
- Tap Battery to see more details.

- Tap Battery usage to view additional information about your battery usage.

- The chart shows the battery level since its last full charge.

- To see battery usage by app, choose View by apps.

- Tap the name of a listed app to view or alter its battery use.

Some apps allow you to limit background battery usage.

To view your battery usage by system function, click View by Systems.

Tip: Rounding can prevent listed amounts from totaling 100%.

See how long it takes to get full charge.

Plug in your phone. Allow time to watch how rapidly it charges.

- Open your phone's Settings app.

- Under "Battery," you can check how much charge remains and how long it will take to charge completely.

How to Add a battery widget to the home screen.

The battery widget displays battery information for your Pixel phone and any nearby connected devices.

To add the battery widget:

- On the Home screen, tap and hold an empty area.
- Tap Widgets.
- Tap the battery.
- Tap and hold the battery widget.
- Slide the widget wherever you want it. Lift your finger.
- To resize the widget, drag the dots.
- Once you're done, tap outside the widget.

How to Turn your Pixel phone on and off.

You can turn your phone on and off using the top button on the right side.

Turn the power on or off.

- To turn on your phone when it is turned off, press and hold the Power button for a few seconds.
- Press and hold the Power button until a buzz sounds (up to 7 seconds in some cases).

To power off your phone while it is turned on:

- Press and hold the Power and Volume Up buttons for a few seconds. Then, on your screen, choose Power Off Power.
- To access the power menu, press and hold the Power button and select Settings. Tap System, and Gestures, and then Press and Hold the Power button. Then choose the Power menu.

54

Once completed, press and hold the power button for a few seconds. Then, on your screen, choose Power Off Power.

Tip: Charge your phone before turning it on.

Turn the screen off and back on.

Press the Power button once to switch on and off your phone's screen while it is active.

Restart (reboot).

Restart the phone.

- Press and hold the Power and Volume Up buttons for a few seconds.
- Tap Restart.

How to Insert a SIM card

With your phone off:

- In the small hole on the phone's left edge, insert the SIM ejection tool.

- Firmly but gently push until the tray comes out.

- Remove the tray and insert the nano SIM card inside.

- Gently push the tray back into the slot.

- You may need to restart your phone to receive mobile service. To restart an active phone, press and hold the power button for approximately 3 seconds. Then, tap Restart.

How to Add apps, shortcuts & widgets to your Home screens

To quickly get to your favorite content, you can customize your Home screens

Add to Home Screens

Add an application.

- Swipe up from the bottom of the home screen.

- Touch and drag the app. You'll discover photos of each Home screen.

- Slide the app to where you want it. Lift your finger.

Add a shortcut.

- Tap and hold the app, then raise your finger. If the app has shortcuts, you'll see a list.
- Touch and hold the shortcut.
- Slide the shortcut wherever you want it. Lift your finger.

TIP: To use a shortcut without adding it to your Home screen, press it.

Add or resize a widget.

Add a widget.

- On the Home screen, tap and hold an empty area.
- Tap Widgets.
- Find the app that includes the widget you're looking for.

- Tap the app to see the widgets that are currently accessible.
- Touch and hold the widget. You'll get photos of your home screens.
- Slide the widget wherever you want it. Lift your finger.

Resize a widget.

- Tap and hold the widget on the Home screen.
- Lift your finger. If the widget can be resized, it will show an outline with dots on the sides.
- To resize the widget, drag the dots.
- When you've finished, tap outside the widget.

Organize on home screens.

Create a folder (or group).

- Tap and hold an application or shortcut.
- Drag one program or shortcut to the top of another. Lift your finger.

- To add more, drag them to the top of the group.
- Tap to name the group. Next, tap the suggested folder name. You can also choose a suggested name from the list at the top of the keyboard or enter your own.

Move an application, shortcut, widget, or group.

- Touch and drag the item. You'll get photos of your home screens.
- Slide the object to where you want it.
- Lift your finger.

Delete an application, shortcut, widget, or group.

- Touch and hold the item.
- Drag the item up to remove it.
- Lift your finger.
- You can choose "Remove," "Uninstall," or both. "Remove" will only remove an app from

your Home screen. "Uninstall" will remove it from your device.

Add a home screen.

- Touch and hold an app, shortcut, or group.
- Slide it to the right until you see a blank Home Screen.
- Lift your finger.

Remove the home screen.

- Remove your apps, shortcuts, widgets, and groups from the Home screen.
- After the last one is deleted, the home screen will be removed.

How to Customize your home screen.

Change information at the top.

The "At A Glance" information appears at the top of your main Home screen. For instance, you can get information about:

- Date

- Daily weather
- What's next on your calendar?
- Nest Package Delivery Reminders
- Flight baggage claim information

To change the information displayed:

- Touch and hold the section.
- Tap Customize, then Settings.

Change an application.

A row of your preferred apps will show at the bottom of your screen.

Remove your favorite application: Select and hold the app you want to delete from your favorites list. Drag it to another part of the screen.

Add your favorite application: Swipe up from the bottom of the screen. Tap and hold the app. Move the app to an empty location in your favorites.

Change the other Home screen settings.

- On your Home screen, tap and hold an empty spot.
- Select Home Settings.

Enable or disable the search bar animations.

Your home screen's search bar may periodically show animations. The animations are only used on exceptional occasions, such as holidays.

- To disable or enable these animations, tap and hold the search bar.
- Tap More and then Preferences.
- Turn the search box effects on and off.

How to Change Your Favorite Apps.

Your favorite apps are displayed at the bottom of the screen. Your phone suggests apps for your favorites based on your most recent and frequently used apps, as well as your habits. Your suggested programs have colored shadows surrounding their icons.

When there is an empty spot in the row, a new suggested app will display. You can pin, delete, or add any of the recommended apps. You can also manually replace any application.

Pin an application.

- Tap and hold the suggested application.
- Tap the pin symbol in the menu's top right corner.

Delete your favorite app.

- Tap and hold the suggested application.
- Tap the pin symbol in the menu's top right corner.
- To remove an app as a suggestion, tap and drag it to "Don't suggest app."

Turn off app suggestions for your favorites.

- On your phone's Home screen, tap and hold an empty spot.
- Tap Home Settings, then Suggestions.
- Decide whether to turn on or off.
- Suggestions for all applications. A list of ideas appears on the home screen.

Add your favorite application.

- Swipe up from the bottom of the screen.
- Tap and hold the app.
- Move the app to a space close to your favorites.
- Lift your finger.

How to Change the wallpaper on your Pixel smartphone.

You can change the background images on your phone's home and lock screens. You can choose your photos or use images from your phone, including ones that update automatically.

Change wallpapers.

- On your phone's Home screen, tap and hold a space.
- Tap Wallpaper and Style. If you do not see "Wallpaper & Style," select Wallpapers.
- Tap Change Wallpaper.
- To use your image, select My Photos.
- To use a curated image, tap the category. Then an image.
- To utilize a live wallpaper, select Bloom or Living Universe. Then a wallpaper. If necessary, tap Download.
- At the bottom, select Set Wallpaper or Done.
- If available, specify which screen(s) will display the wallpaper.

Create special effects for photo wallpapers

- On your phone's Home screen, tap and hold an empty spot.
- Tap Wallpaper and then My Photos.

- Select a photo.
- Tap Effects.
- Turn on Create Cinematic Wallpaper.
- To view your wallpaper, go to the Home screen and choose Lock screen.
- To change the wallpaper location, select Home screen, Lock screen, or both.

Make personalized wallpapers

- Select one emoji or get a random assortment:
- On your phone's Home screen, tap and hold an empty spot.
- Tap Wallpaper & Style, followed by Change Wallpaper and Emoji Workshop.
- Tap Edit Emoji in the bottom right corner, then Done.
- Select an emoji.

For one specific emoji: Select from the keyboard. You can use up to 14 emojis to personalize your wallpaper.

For a random assortment: Tap Randomize.

- Select a pattern and size.
- In the bottom panel, pick Patterns.
- Select a pattern style.
- Use the slider to adjust the size of the emojis on the pattern.
- Choose a color.
- Tap the Colours option in the bottom panel.
- Select a background color.
- Preview and set your wallpaper.
- To preview your emoji wallpaper, tap the Lock screen and then the Home screen.
- When you're satisfied with your preview, tap Set Wallpaper.
- To change the wallpaper position, select Home screen or Home and lock screens.

Create AI wallpapers

Generative AI allows you to create personalized and unique wallpapers based on your prompts. You can do this:

- Fill in the blanks to construct a prompt based on a pre-written template.
- Choose several options to fine-tune the final effect.
- You can save your produced wallpapers for later use.

To make an AI wallpaper:

- On your phone's Home screen, tap and hold an empty spot.
- Tap Wallpaper & Style, then More Wallpapers, and finally AI Wallpaper.
- Select a theme for your AI-generated wallpaper.
- Tap Inspire Me to get a random wallpaper for your chosen prompt.

- Tap any underlined word in the prompt to see particular possibilities.
- Tap Create Wallpaper to begin the wallpaper creation process.
- Swiping left or right lets you select from several AI-generated backgrounds.
- To change the wallpaper, first press Done, then Lock screen or Home screen, and lastly Set wallpaper.

Tip: Once used, the wallpaper is saved and can be reused again.

Change the clock style to the latest Android version.

- On your phone's Home screen, tap and hold an empty spot.
- Tap Wallpaper and Style, then Lock Screen.
- To see the style options, swipe left or right over the caption "Clock color and size."
- Tap Colour and select your desired color.

Tip: Use the slider to make the color paler or darker.

- Tap Size and select the size you require.
- The clock's size varies depending on the lock screen content and is modest.
- To save your style changes, use the left arrow.

Change the Home Screen Styles

To personalize your Home screen's fonts, icons, shapes, and colors:

- On your phone's Home screen, tap and hold an empty spot.
- Tap Wallpaper and Style.
- Choose Wallpaper or Basic colors.
- Choose a style.
- Tap Apply or Done.

Change the Home Screen Grid

To choose a grid size from your Home screen:

- On your phone's Home screen, tap and hold an empty spot.

- Tap Wallpaper and Style.

- At the bottom, choose App grid.

- Choose a grid size.

- Tap Done.

Use theme icons.

Change the supported app icons to match your phone's color scheme:

- On your phone's Home screen, tap and hold an empty spot.

- Tap Wallpaper and Style.

- To enable or disable the themed icons, tap them at the bottom.

How to Use gestures with your Pixel phone.

You can interact with your phone through gestures. You can toggle some gestures on and off.

Turn gestures on and off.

- Launch your phone's Settings app.
- Tap System, then Gestures.
- Tap the gesture that you want to change.

Check notifications.

- Swipe your fingerprint to receive notifications.
- Swiping down on your Pixel phone's fingerprint sensor when it's unlocked allows you to check your notifications.

Tap to check the phone.

When your phone is locked, you may see your notifications by tapping the screen.

Lift to check your phone.

Simply pick up your locked phone to check for alerts.

Find your applications.

Find recent applications.

Swipe up from the bottom of the screen and hold it.
When you feel a vibration, let it pass.

Find every application.

Swipe up from the bottom of your screen.

Quick Tap to open an app or finish a task.

Two taps on the rear of your phone will allow you to snap a screenshot or play and pause media. You can also see notifications or run an app. To change your settings:

- Open your phone's Settings app.
- Go to System, Gestures, and Quick Tap.
- Turn on Use Quick Tap.

- Choose an action.
- To launch an app, select Open app. Next to "Open app," click Settings. Then, select an application.
- To complete the motion, double-tap your phone's back.

Open or switch between cameras.

To open your camera from any screen, tap the power button twice.

Flip cameras

Twisting your phone twice when the camera is open switches between the front and back cameras.

Quickly mute your phone.

- Turn on vibrate or mute.
- To enable vibrate or mute while preventing ringing, use the power and volume up buttons.

Flip to Shhh.

To rapidly enable Do Not Disturb, place your phone face down on a flat surface.

Talk to your assistance.

- To launch Google Assistant using gesture navigation, swipe from the right or left corner of your screen.
- Push and hold the power button.

How to Find and set up devices near you.

Using your Pixel phone, you can find and connect to nearby devices.

Set up new devices around you.

Step one: Set up your phone.

If you haven't already, use your phone:

- Turn on Bluetooth.
- Turn on Location.
- If you disabled device notifications, enable them.

Step 2: Set up the new device.

You can connect Wear OS watches, other Android phones and tablets, and Fast Pair-compatible accessories. Accessories that work with fast pair are clearly labeled on their boxes. Many also use the phrase "Made by Google" or "Made for Google." Google Store offers a variety of accessories.

- Turn on a new device that has not yet been set up. Put the device into pairing mode.
- Turn on the phone's screen.
- A notification will appear on your phone, offering to set up the new device.
- Tap the notification.
- Follow the onscreen instructions.

Switch notifications on or off.

By default, you will receive notifications about nearby devices, which you can customize. If you turn off notifications, you may still locate nearby devices by opening your phone's Settings app.

- Open your phone's Settings app.
- Tap Google, followed by Devices & Sharing, and finally Devices.
- Turn Scan for Nearby Devices on or off.

How to Change your screen color at night on a Pixel phone

Adjust the screen colors to save battery life and make it easier to use in low light conditions. The Dark theme, Night Light, and Grayscale settings on your phone can help you use it at night and fall asleep more easily.

Automatically darken your phone's background and applications.

To darken your phone's background, use the Dark theme. You can set the Dark theme to activate every night.

- Launch your Settings app.
- Tap Display, then Dark Theme.
- Tap Schedule.

Choose Turns on at a specific time, from sunset to sunrise, or at bedtime.

- Launch your phone's Settings app.

- Tap Display and then Dark Theme.
- Tap Schedule and then Turn it on at bedtime.

Tip: To prevent the Dark theme from activating automatically, select Schedule and then None.

Automatically dim your phone's wallpaper.

- Open your phone's Settings app.
- Tap Digital Wellbeing and Parental Controls.
- Select Bedtime Mode.
- Turn on the Bedtime Mode.
- Tap Customise, and then Screen alternatives for bedtime.
- Turn on the dim wallpaper.

Automatically switch your screen to Night Light or Amber.

You may lessen the blue tint on your phone's screen to make it easier to operate in low-light situations. Blue light may make it difficult to fall asleep. Night Light allows you to make your screen red or amber, allowing your eyes to acclimatize to night vision more easily.

- Open your phone's Settings app.
- Tap Display and then Night Light.
- Tap Schedule to choose your start and end times.
- Tap turns on at a specific moment. Then specify your "start time" and "end time."
- Tap turns on from sunset to sunrise. If you turn off location services, sunset-to-sunrise scheduling will fail.
- To prevent night mode from being activated automatically, select Schedule And then None.

Automatically change your screen to grayscale

To help you rest at night, turn your phone's screen to black and white.

- Open your phone's Settings app.
- Tap Digital Wellbeing and Parental Controls.

- Select Bedtime mode.
- Switch on bedtime mode.
- tap Customize, and then Screen alternatives for bedtime.
- Turn on grayscale.

Tip: Quick Settings on your phone provide access to the Dark theme, Night Light, and Bedtime mode.

Change your theme yourself.

If you want to modify the settings, you can turn the themes on and off at any moment.

- Open your phone's Settings app.
- Tap the display button.
- Tap your screen's color option.
- Under "Appearance," select the Dark theme.
- Under "Color," enable Night Light.

How to Find and delete files from a Pixel phone.

Your downloaded files are usually stored in the Files app on your Pixel phone.

Find and open files on your Pixel phone.

- Open your device's Files app.
- The file categories will show.
- To sort by name, date, or size, choose a file category, then More, and then Sort by.
- To open a file, tap it.

Delete files from your Pixel phone.

- Open your device's Files app.
- Tap a category, then a file.
- Tap Delete, then move one file to Trash.

CONTACT

How to Add, move, or import contacts.

Google Contacts lets you save names, email addresses, phone numbers, and more.

Add a contact.

- Launch the Contacts app.
- Tap the "Add Question" button in the bottom right corner.
- Enter the contact's name, email, or phone number.
- Select the account in which you want to save the contact. Tap the Down Arrow button next to your email address.
- To enter further name details: Next to "Name," hit the Down arrow.
- To add a photo: At the top, click Add Picture. Take or select a photo, and then hit Choose.

- To include additional information, like a street address or notes: Tap More Fields.
- When you're finished, tap Save.

Import contacts.

You can link all of your contacts to your Google account. After importing, the contacts will remain in your other account.

From the SIM card

If you have contacts stored on your SIM card, you can import them into your Google account.

Insert the SIM card into your device.

- Launch the Contacts app.
- At the bottom, select Fix & Manage Import from SIM.
- If you have multiple accounts on your device, choose which one you wish to save your contacts in.

From a VCF file.

If you have saved your contacts as a VCF file, you can import them into your Google account.

- Launch the Contacts app.
- At the bottom, choose Fix & Manage Import from File.
- If you have multiple accounts on your device, choose which one you wish to save your contacts in.

- Find and pick the VCF file you wish to import.

Move a contact.

You can move contacts from other accounts to Google Accounts.

Moving a contact deletes it from the original account.

- Launch the Contacts app.
- Select a contact.
- In the upper right corner, tap Menu More. Transfer to another account.
- Select which Google account you wish to transfer the contact to.

Merge duplicate contacts.

Merge numerous listings for the same person in Google Contacts.

Duplicate entries should be merged.

- Launch the Contacts app.

- In the top right corner, select the Google Account containing the duplicate contacts you want to consolidate.
- Tap the Merge & Fix button at the bottom.
- Tap Merge Duplicates. If you do not see this option, it means there are no contacts to merge.
- To accept a single duplicate contact recommendation, choose Merge.
- To accept all duplicate contact suggestions, scroll to the bottom of the screen and tap Merge.

Optional: If you'd like to determine which contacts to merge:

- Open your Contacts app.
- Tap the More Select icon in the top right corner.
- Select which contacts you wish to integrate.
- In the upper right corner, select More Merge.
- Separate the merged contacts.

How to Export, backup, and restore contacts.

You can use your computer to transfer contacts to a different email account.

You can back up the contacts on your phone or SIM card. If you lose or need to replace your phone, you can use the new phone to restore your contacts.

If you save your contacts to your Google Account, they will be available on your phone once you sign in. You will not need to restore contacts this way.

Export your contacts.

- Launch the Contacts app.
- At the bottom, choose Fix & Manage, then Export to File.
- Choose one or more accounts to export contacts from.
- Tap Export to.VCF file.

Turn the automatic backup feature off or on.

When you first set up your Google Account on your phone, you will be asked if you wish to backup your data. To change this setting:

- Open your phone's Settings app.
- Tap System, then Backup.
- Turn Back Up to Google Drive on or off.

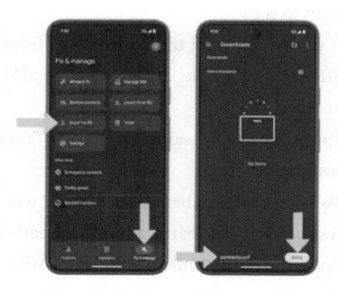

Restore contacts from backups.

- Open your phone's Settings app.

- Tap Google.

- Tap Setup and Restore.

- Tap Restore Contacts.

- If you have several Google accounts, choose which account's contacts to recover by pressing From account.

- Tap the phone that contains the contacts you want to copy.

- If you do not want to copy contacts from your SIM card or phone storage, disable SIM card or device storage.

- Tap Restore and wait until you see "Contacts restored."

- To avoid duplicates, your phone will only restore contacts that it does not already have. Your restored contacts will sync with your current Google Account and other devices.

How to Edit or delete contacts.

After you've added contacts to your Android device, you can edit or delete them.

Change contact information.

- On your Android device, launch the Contacts app.
- Tap the contact you wish to edit.
- Tap the Edit button in the top right corner.
- If asked, select an account.
- Enter the contact's name, email address, and telephone number.
- To add more information, tap More fields or the Down arrow.
- To change a contact's photo, tap it and select an option.
- Select Save.

Add a contact to your favorites.

You can move persons you contact frequently to the top of your list.

- Launch the Contacts app.
- Tap the contact you want to add to your favorites.
- At the top, select Favourite.

Delete contacts.

- Launch the Contacts app.
- Select an option.
- **Single contact:** Tap it. Tap More in the upper right corner, then delete.
- To add multiple contacts, touch and hold one before tapping the others.
- Tap Delete and then Delete.
- **All contacts:** Tap More in the upper right corner, followed by Select All, Delete, and lastly Delete.

To permanently delete contacts in the trash:

- **Single contact:** Tap the contact and select Delete forever.

- **Multiple contacts**: To add multiple contacts, touch and hold one before tapping the others.

- Tap More, then Delete Forever, and finally Delete Forever.

- **All contacts:** Tap Empty Trash, then Delete Forever.

Recover Deleted Contacts.

If you removed a contact within the last 30 days, you can remove it from your trash.

To access Trash, you must have automatic sync turned on.

Trash can only be accessed when your device is online. If your device is disconnected or does not have a network connection, it will not load until you reconnect.

- On your Android device, open the Google Contacts app.

- In the top right corner, select the Google Account that is linked with the contact you moved to the trash.

- At the bottom, choose Fix & Manage, then Trash.

Select an option.

- **Single contact**: Tap the contact, then select Recover.

- **Multiple contacts**: Touch and hold one contact, then tap the remaining contacts.

- Tap More and then Recover.

- **All contacts:** tap More, then Select All, More, and Recover.

Undo changes to contacts.

You can undo any modifications you made to your contacts during the past 30 days all at once.

- Launch the Contacts app.

- Tap your profile image in the top right corner, then select Contacts app settings.
- Under "Edit contacts," choose Undo changes. If prompted, choose which Google Account you want to modify.
- Select a time to return to.
- Tap Confirm.

Tip: If you restore contacts to a certain period, such as one week ago, all contacts added after that time will be excluded

Block contacts

When you block a number, you will no longer receive calls or texts from it. If a contact has multiple phone numbers, each one will be blocked.

- Launch the Contacts app.
- Tap the contact you want to block.
- Tap More in the upper right corner, then Block numbers and Block.

- Pressing on a single number will only block that number.
- Spam Caller: Select "Report as Spam."
- To unblock a contact, select More, Unblock numbers, and then Unblock.

View the blocked numbers.

- Launch the Contacts app.

- At the bottom, choose Fix & Manage, then Blocked numbers.

How to View, organize, and share contacts.

Contacts allow you to organize people and businesses by label.

The contact app lets you search for someone's contact information or organize connections by labeling them as "friends" or "family."

Check your contacts.

- Launch the Contacts app.
- At the bottom, pick Contacts.

Contacts By Label:

- At the top, pick Label.
- Select a label.

Contacts for another account:

Tap the profile image in the top right corner, and then select an account.

Contacts for all of your accounts:

- At the top, select your account and then All contacts.

Tip: If you have numerous contacts with identical information, they will be consolidated into a single contact.

Contact someone.

You can reach out to your contacts by phone, email, or text.

- Launch the Contacts app.
- Select a contact from the list.
- Choose an option.

Form a group.

Contacts can be grouped with labels.

- Launch the Contacts app.
- At the top, select Label, followed by New Label.
- Enter a label name.
- Tap OK.
- Add one contact to a label:
- Tap Add Contact.

- Select a contact.

- Add many contacts to a label.

- Tap Add Contact.

- Touch and hold a contact.

- Tap Other Contacts, then Add.

Tip: If a contact has numerous email addresses, only the default address is added to the label group.

Change the default email address.

- Open the Contacts app on your Android device and pick the contact.

- Tap and hold the email address.

- Tap Set default.

Delete contacts from a group.

- Launch the Contacts app.

- Tap the Label symbol in the upper-left corner.

- Select a label.

- Tap More and then Remove Contacts.

- Tap the Remove button next to the contact you'd like to erase.

Share your contacts!

- Launch the Contacts app.
- Tap one of the contacts from the list.
- Tap More in the upper right corner, followed by Share.
- Decide how you want to share the contact.

Check your contact details.

- Tap your profile image in the top right corner, then select Contacts app settings.
- Tap your information.

How to Backup and sync your device's contacts.

Some contacts from your phone may not be preserved in Google Contacts. For example, some apps save contacts in device storage, limiting their management to that device. Changes you make to these contacts will not be synchronized across Google services or other signed-in devices. If the gadget is misplaced or destroyed, these contacts could be lost.

Device contacts can be automatically saved as Google contacts for backup and synchronization across all of your devices. Google contacts are accessible through all Google services and can be handled from any signed-in device. If the original device is lost or destroyed, the contacts will be instantly transferred to a new device when you sign in.

Backup and sync your device's contacts.

Backup and sync device contacts by storing them in Google Contacts.

- On your Android phone, open the "Settings" app.
- Tap Google, followed by Settings for Google apps, Google Contacts sync, Also sync device

contacts, and Automatically backup and sync device contacts.

- Enable Automatic backup and sync device contacts.

- Choose the account you wish to save your contacts to. Contacts are only automatically saved to one Google Account.

How to Turn Google Contacts sync on or off.

Turning off Google Contacts sync will remove your contacts from your device. To replace them, reactivate Google Contacts sync.

You will lose any changes you made on your device that have not yet been synced to the cloud. To ensure that these changes are saved to the cloud, manually sync using the instructions below before turning off Google Contacts sync:

- Open your Android phone settings.

- Tap Google, then All Services, and finally Settings for Google apps.
- Tap Google Contacts Sync, then Status.
- Turn Google Contacts syncing on or off.

Turn off automatic synchronization.

If you want Google Contacts on your device but don't want your changes to be synced automatically to the cloud, you can disable automatic sync.

- On your Android phone, launch the Settings app.
- Tap Passwords & Accounts.
- Choose your Google account.
- If there are numerous accounts, choose the one with the settings you want to alter.
- Tap Account Sync.
- Turn Contacts off.

Sync your contacts manually.

If automatic sync is turned off and you wish to update your contacts, you can manually sync Google Contacts.

- open the Settings app.
- Tap Google, then All Services, and then Settings for Google Apps.
- Tap Google Contacts Sync, then Status.
- Tap Refresh.

This can also be done through Google's Contacts app.

- Launch the Contact app.
- To sync, drag down the contacts list.

HOW TO MAKE & RECEIVE PHONE CALLS

You can make phone calls using the Phone app and other apps or widgets that display your contacts.

When you see a phone number, you can usually tap it to dial.

Make a telephone call

- Launch your Phone app.
- Decide who to call.
- To enter a number, press Dialpad.
- Tap Contacts to choose one of your stored contacts. We may offer suggested contacts depending on your call history.
- Tap Recents to select numbers that you have recently called.
- Tap Favorites to select contacts that have been saved there.
- Tap Call.

- When you've concluded the call, press End Call. If your call is minimized, drag the call bubble to the lower right corner of the screen.

Answer or reject a phone call.

When you get a call, the caller's phone number, contact name, or caller ID details are displayed on the screen. When Google can verify a phone number, it displays the Verified indicator above the caller's name or number.

- To answer a call while your phone is locked, swipe the white circle to the top of the screen or press Answer.
- To reject a call while your phone is locked, swipe the white circle to the bottom of the screen or tap Dismiss. Rejected callers might leave a message.
- To reject the call and send a text message to the caller, swipe up from the Message icon New message.

Tips:

- When you answer one call while on another, you put the current one on hold.
- If Google Assistant is enabled, you can answer or decline calls with your voice. Simply say, "Hey Google, answer the call."

"Hey Google, reject the call."

Use the phone calling options.

While the call is open:

- To access the keypad, select Dialpad.
- Tap the Speaker to toggle between the earpiece, speakerphone, and any Bluetooth headsets that are currently connected.
- To muffle or unmute your microphone, tap Mute.
- To pause a chat without disconnecting, press Hold. To continue the call, touch Hold again.

- To switch between current calls, hit Switch. Others are put on hold.

- Tap Call merge to combine all of your existing calls into a single conference call.

- To end the call, navigate to the Home screen.

- Drag the call bubble to your chosen destination.

- To conceal the call bubble, drag it to the bottom of the screen and choose "Hide".

- Switch to a video call using specific carriers and devices. Tap Video Call.

Transfer an active call to a different number.

- While you are on an active call, tap Add Call.

- Enter a phone number.

- Tap Call.

- When the call connects, select Transfer. Your call is routed to the number you specified in Step 2.

How to Make calls via Wi-Fi.

In some cases, you can call people using a Wi-Fi connection rather than a mobile carrier.

Before you can make calls over Wi-Fi, you must enable the feature in your settings.

Turn on Wi-Fi calling.

Use your mobile carrier's Wi-Fi calling.

- Open the Phone application.

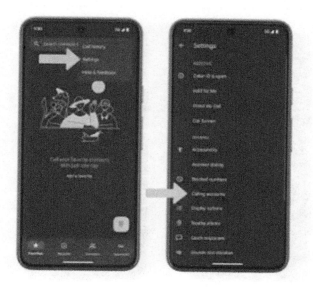

- Tap More, then Settings.

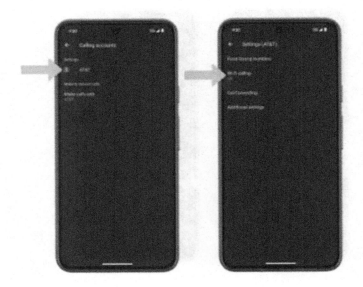

- Tap Calls.
- Tap Wi-Fi Calling.

How to View and delete call history.

You can view a list of calls you've placed, answered, or missed. And you can remove calls from that list.

View your call history.

- Open your device's Phone app.
- Tap Recents.

Each call on your list will display one or more of the following icons:

- Missed calls
- Calls you answered
- outgoing calls.

See the call details.

- To get more information about a call in your history, tap it and then Call for more information.
- You'll see information on each call made to that number, including when it happened, how long it lasted, and whether it was inbound or outgoing.

Add numbers to your contact list.

Tap the call in your call history to add the number to your contacts. Add current contacts or add new ones.

Delete a call from your history.

- Open your device's Phone app.
- Tap Recents.
- Tap a number or contact.
- Tap Call Details.
- At the top, pick Trash Delete.

Delete your full call history.

- Open your device's Phone app.
- Tap Recents.
- Tap More and then Call History.
- Tap the More option, then Clear Call History.
- When prompted whether you wish to remove your call history, select OK.

How to Check your Voicemail

You can listen to your voicemail by dialing your voicemail service. Some devices and carriers let you access a list of your voicemails in the Phone app.

How to Check your Voicemail

- Tap the message notice.

117

- When you receive a voicemail, you can check it using the notification on your phone.
- Swipe down from the top of the screen.
- Tap Voicemail.

Call your voicemail.

Call your voicemail service and check your messages.

- Open the Phone app.
- At the bottom, click Dialpad.
- Touch and hold one.

Change your voicemail settings.

- Open the Phone app.
- In the upper right corner, select More options.
- Tap Settings, then Voicemail.
- You can change the carrier that handles your voicemail messages. Tap Advanced Settings, then Service.

- Set up your voicemail. Tap Advanced Settings, then Setup.

- Change your notification settings: Tap Notifications.

- Turn on the vibration. Tap Notifications, Advanced, and then Vibrations.

How to Use more Phone app features

How to Use caller ID and spam protection.

When you make or receive a call with caller ID and spam protection enabled, you can receive information about callers or businesses that are not in your contact list, as well as warnings about potential spam callers.

If someone from outside your contact list calls you or you call them, Google receives the phone number to help identify its business Caller ID name or determine whether the call is spam.

Disable or re-enable caller ID and spam protection.

These features are turned on by default. You can turn it off.

Caller ID and spam protection may need your phone to report call details to Google. It does not influence whether your phone number appears when you make a call.

- On your device, open the Phone app.
- Tap More Options. More, then Settings, Spam, and Call Screen.
- Turn Enable or disable caller and spam ID.

Optional: To ban spam calls on your phone, tap "Filter spam calls." You do not receive missed calls or voicemail notifications, but filtered calls are displayed in your call history, and you may access your voicemail.

Turn on the caller ID announcements.

Turn on the Caller ID announcement to hear the name or number of incoming calls.

- On your device, open the Phone app.

- Tap More Options. More, followed by Settings, Caller ID announcement, and finally Declare caller ID.

Choose an option.

- Always
- Only while using a headset.
- Never

Mark calls as spam

You can flag all calls from a single number as spam to prevent future calls and report the spammer.

- On your device, open the Phone app.
- At the bottom, pick Recents.
- Tap the call that you want to report as spam.
- Tap Block or Report Spam.

Tip: Tap and hold the call that you want to report as spam. Then, tap Block or Report Spam.

Recognize spam

If you see "Suspected spam caller" or "Spam" on the caller ID, the call could be spam. You can choose to answer the call or block and report the phone number.

Report an error in spam protection.

If a call from someone you know is erroneously labeled as spam, you can report it. Future calls from this number will not be flagged as spam.

- On your device, open the Phone app.
- Tap Recent Calls.
- Tap the call that was wrongly flagged as spam.
- Tap Unblock and then Unblock.

Verify or share the caller ID.

You can now share information about companies you call or who call you. Information can:

- Enter a business name or category.
- Be displayed during incoming calls.

- Assist people in learning more about the mission of their company, institution, or group.

Confirm or suggest a new caller ID.

- On your device, open the Phone app.
- At the bottom, pick Recents.
- Tap Was it a business? or Caller ID feedback, and then follow the instructions.
- Tap Submit.
- If you confirm that the phone number is not a business number, no information will be sent to Google.
- The information you enter will not reveal any personally identifiable information.

Change your selection after providing feedback:

- In the Recents tab, tap and hold the call you want to use.
- Select "Send Feedback."

124

How to Use the Phone app to record calls.

To record phone calls:

- launch the Phone app.
- Tap More options in the upper right corner, then Settings, and finally Call recording.
- Under "Always record," select Numbers not in your contacts.
- Tap Always record.

Turn on "Always record" for selected contacts.

Important: You are responsible for adhering to all laws regarding phone recording. Use call recording responsibly and only when necessary.

- launch the Phone app.
- Tap More options in the upper right corner, then Settings, and finally Call recording.
- Under "Always record," select Selected numbers.

- Turn on "Always record selected numbers."
- Tap the Add button in the top right corner.
- Select a contact.
- Tap Always record.
- **(Optional):** Repeat these procedures for each contact you want to record.

Tip: Open a contact to enable call recording. Tap Edit contact in the bottom right corner of the contact card, then select Always record calls.

Begin recording from a call.

Important: The first time you record a call, you will be informed that you must adhere to local recording laws. Many jurisdictions need all participants to agree before recording a call.

To preserve all users' privacy, when you start recording, both participants are notified that the call is being recorded. When you stop recording, both parties are notified that the call is no longer being recorded.

- Open the Phone app.
- Make or receive a call.
- On the current call screen, tap Record
- To end the recording, select Stop recording. Stop recording.
- Keep in mind that deleting a call log also removes the corresponding call recording.

Find a recorded call.

Your recordings are private and retained on your smartphone. Calls are not saved or backed up from the device.

To locate the recording:

- Open the Phone app.
- Tap Recents.
- Tap on the caller you taped.
- If you have recorded the most recent call, select the player from the "Recents" page.
- If you recorded a prior call, select History. Then, select a recording from the list of calls.

- Tap the play button.
- Optional: To share a recorded call, choose Share.

Tip: You can send recorded calls to compatible apps such as email or messaging.

Decide how long to keep recorded calls.

Important: You are responsible for following all rules governing phone recording. Record calls responsibly and only when necessary. Currently, automated call recording is only accessible in India.

- open the Phone app.
- In the upper right corner, hit More options. More, followed by Settings. Call recording.
- Click the Delete button under "Recordings."
- Decide how long you wish to keep a recorded call before it is automatically removed.
- Tap Confirm.
- **Optional:** Tap Delete all recordings now, then delete.

Delete a recorded call.

- Open the Phone app.
- Tap Recents.
- Locate the number or contact for the recorded call you wish to remove.
- Tap History.
- Swipe left on the recording in the call list.

How to Use Hold for me.

When you phone a business and are put on hold, your Google Assistant can wait for you and alert you when the support representative is available to speak with you. After your call, you can share the audio and transcript to help improve Hold for Me.

Switch the setting on or off.

Important: Once the setting is enabled, you must also enable Hold for Me on each call to allow the Google Assistant to wait for you.

- Open the Phone app.

- Tap More and then Settings.
- Tap Hold for me.
- Switch Hold for Me on or off.
- When you're on the phone, turn on Hold for Me.

Important:

- Hold for Me may not detect when a representative returns to the call in all circumstances.
- Hold For Me stops you from playing music or other audio.

Turn off your phone's silence or vibrate mode.

- Open the Phone app.
- Place a call to a business.
- When you're on hold, tap Hold for me and then Start.
- While you're on hold, you'll see a card on the screen that says "Don't hang up".

- When the support professional is ready to speak with you, a prompt will appear stating "Someone is waiting to speak with you."
- Tap Return to Call.

Share the data from your call.

- Open the Phone app.
- At the bottom, pick Recents.
- Tap Help Us. Improve appears underneath the call log item, followed by Yes, Continue, and Continue.
- If you wish to provide feedback, please enter it in the text box.
- Tap Send.

Tip: To share your data without providing your email address, go to the Send Feedback screen, press the Down arrow next to the "From" field, and then pick Google user.

How to Use Direct My Call.

When you call a business with an automated menu, Direct My Call displays both the automated voice and the menu options available through the tappable number buttons. Tap the buttons on the screen to select a menu item.

When making a call from a Pixel, you may see menu options before speaking.

- The "Faster menu options" feature is turned on by default.
- To turn it off, launch the Phone app and pick More, Settings, and Direct My Call. Then, disable "Faster menu options".

Turn Direct My Call on and off.

- Open the Phone app.
- In the upper right corner, tap More, then Settings.
- Click "Direct My Call."
- Turn Direct My Call on and off.

132

Tip: To exit Direct My Call while on an active phone call, touch Close in the upper left corner of the screen.

Share the data from your call.

After your call, you can share the audio and transcript to help enhance Direct My Call.

- Open the Phone app.
- At the bottom, pick Recents.
- Tap Help us improve this beneath the call log entry, then click Continue.
- Optional: You can leave feedback in the text box.
- Tap the Send button in the upper-right corner.

Tip: To share your data without providing your email address, go to the Send Feedback screen, press the Down arrow next to the "From" field, and then pick Google user.

How to Screen your calls before answering them.

Before you answer the phone, use the Call Screen to see who is calling and why. Call Screen works on your device and does not require Wi-Fi or mobile data.

Enable automatic call screening on your phone.

To enable automatic call screening:

Open the Phone application.

Tap More, then Settings, Spam, or Call Screen.

Tap the Call Screen.

Choose your protection level:

- **Protection Level:** Toggle Turn automatic call screening on or off.
- Spam
- Possibly faked numbers.
- First-time callers

How to Change Phone app settings

Change the call settings.

You can customize your phone's ringtone, vibration settings, quick responses, and call history display.

How to Change the sound and vibration settings.

- Open the Phone app.
- Tap More and then Settings.
- Tap Sounds and Vibrations.
- Tap Phone Ringtone to choose one of the available ringtones.
- To have your phone vibrate when you receive a call, select Also vibrate for calls.
- To hear noises when you tap the dial pad, go to Dial pad tones. (If you don't see "Dial pad tones," choose Keypad tones.)

Change the way callers' names are formatted and displayed.

- Open the Phone app.
- Tap More and then Settings.
- Tap Display Options.
- To modify the way your phone sorts calls in your history, tap Sort By.
- Tap Name format to change how your phone displays contact names in your history.

Change the text replies.

If you are unable to answer a phone call, you can send an automated text message. Here's how to personalize your automated SMS messages.

- Open the Phone app.
- Tap More and then Settings.
- Tap Quick Responses.
- Select a response from the list.
- Edit the response.
- Tap OK.

How to Turn Clear Calling on or off.

- Open your phone's Settings app.
- Tap Sound and Vibrations, then Clear Calling.
- Turn Turn Clear Calling on and off.

How to Block and unblock phone numbers.

If you don't want to receive calls from a particular phone number, you can block it. When the number attempts to call you, your phone will automatically decline it.

Block a number.

- Open the Phone application.
- Tap More and then Call History.
- Tap a call from the number you want to block.

- Tap Block/Report Spam.

Blocking Unknown Numbers

- Open the Phone application.

- Tap more.

- Tap Settings and then Blocked numbers.

- Turn on Unknown.

- This blocks calls from private or unknown numbers. You will continue to receive calls from phone numbers that do not appear in your contacts.

Unblock a number.

- Open the Phone application.
- Tap more.
- Tap Settings and then Blocked numbers.
- Tap Clear next to the number you wish to unblock, then Unblock.

MESSAGE

Google Messages lets you send and receive texts, images, voice messages, and videos.

How to set up your message app

Make Google Messages your default messaging app.

If your smartphone supports several messaging apps, you can make Google Messages your default messaging app. When you make Google Messages your default messaging app, you may browse your text message history while only sending and receiving new messages from there.

Make Google Messages your default messaging app by choosing one of the following options:

- Open Google Messages.
- When prompted to change your default messaging app, follow the on-screen instructions.

143

Alternatively:

- Open the Settings menu.
- Click Apps.
- In the app list, choose Google Messages, then SMS, and finally Google Messages.
- If you no longer want Google Messages to be your default messaging app, you can delete it or modify the settings on your smartphone.

How to Start a chat with one of your contacts.

If you already have a contact on your phone, it will appear in Google Messages. You can also create new contacts from within the app.

- Open Google Messages.
- Tap Start a conversation.
- Enter the recipient's name, phone number, and/or email address.
- Enter your message and then tap.

Add a new phone number to your chat list as a contact.

- Open Google Messages.
- Choose an ongoing chat with someone who is not in your contacts.
- Tap More and then Add Contact.

Make a new contact from a group conversation.

- Open Google Messages.
- Choose a group chat that contains the phone number you want to add as a contact.
- Tap More and then Details.
- Tap the number you wish to add, then choose Add Contact.

Change the notification settings for specific individuals.

- Open Google Messages.

- Start a discussion with the person you wish to adjust the notifications for.
- Tap More, then Details, and finally Notifications.
- You can block or enable notifications for this person, as well as configure sophisticated notification settings on your device.

How to Send and receive texts.

Send and read text and voice messages with Google Messages.

Google Messages allows you to send and receive text messages with your friends and contacts.

Start a conversation.

Open Google Messages.

Tap Compose.

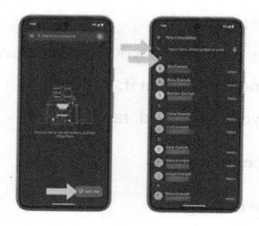

In "To," enter the names, phone numbers, or email addresses you want to message

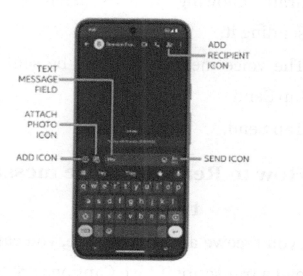

ADD
RECIPIENT
ICON

TEXT
MESSAGE
FIELD

ATTACH
PHOTO
ICON

ADD ICON

SEND ICON

- Send a message
- Tap the message box.
- Enter a message. If you want to save it as a draft and then return it, tap Back
- When you're finished, tap Send

Send a voice message.

- Tap the message box.
- Tap the microphone.
- Make a recording of your voice message.
- The voice message is automatically saved as a draft, allowing you to listen to it before sending it.
- The voice message will not be sent until you tap Send
- Tap Send.

How to Read the voice message transcripts.

When you receive a voice message, you can listen to it or read a transcript if Live Captions are turned off.

- Open Google Messages.
- Open the chat in which you received the voice message.
- At the top of the voice message recording, select View transcript.

How to Read text messages.

To read a message you recently got, swipe down from the top of your screen and select New Message.

You can also open and read a discussion in Google Messages.

Mark messages as read or unread.

Mark each message as read. Tap the More button, and then mark everything as read.

Mark a message as unread.

- In the conversation history, tap and hold the conversation you wish to designate as unread.
- At the top, tap More, then Mark as Unread.

Play a video or a recording.

- Tap a discussion to play a video or recording.
- Next to the video or recording, pick Play.

Call someone while using Google Messages.

- Tap a conversation to initiate a call.
- Tap the Call icon in the upper-right corner.

Read the archived messages.

- To read archived messages, navigate to your conversations list.
- Tap More, then Archived.

Send images, videos, and audio messages using Google Messages.

Google Messages supports MMS, allowing you to send and receive images, videos, audio files, and GIFs.

To send or receive files, grant Google Messages access. Maintain control over your app's permissions.

Send photos, videos, files, and GIFs.

- Open Google Messages.
- Open or initiate a conversation.
- Tap Attach to add a question.
- Select a file.
- Tap Send.

Send voice messages.

- Open Google Messages.
- Start or initiate a conversation.
- Press and hold the microphone.
- Keep a record of your message.
- Tap Send.
- To cancel a voice message in the chat, swipe left or close it.

Send us your location.

- Open Google Messages.
- Start or initiate a conversation.
- Tap Attach.

Archive, delete and read conversations in Google Messages.

You can archive old or unwanted conversations, mark them as read or delete them from Google Messages.

- Open Google Messages.
- Touch and hold each conversation you wish to archive or delete.
- Tap Archive to save the selected conversations in your archives. Archived conversations disappear from the Home screen, but they can still be read.

Mark all as read: Tap the More button, and then Mark all as read.

delete: In Google Messages, select the conversations you wish to erase and hit Delete. If you use Google Messages as your primary messaging app, any deleted chats will be removed from your smartphone. You cannot recover a deleted chat or message.

Manage conversations.

Manage messages within a conversation.

- Open Google Messages.
- Touch and hold a message during a conversation.
- Choose an option.

Share on social media: Tap Share.

See additional information: Tap Information

Copy this message's text: Tap Copy

Forward: To forward a message to another individual, tap Forward.

Delete this message: Select Delete.

Save an attachment, like a photo or sticker. Select Save.

Put conversations back on the home screen.

You may bring archived chats back to the Home screen.

- Open Google Messages.
- Tap More, then Archive.
- Touch and hold each chat you want to recover.
- Tap Unarchive.

Block senders and report spam via Google Messages.

You can block texts from someone in Google texts.

Block a conversation.

- Open Google Messages.
- On the Home screen, tap and hold the communication you want to block.

- Tap Block and then OK.

Unblock a conversation.

Open Google Messages.

Tap your profile photo or icon, then More Options.
More, then Spam, and blocked.

Choose a contact from the list.

Tap Unblock.

Otherwise, tap back.

How to Change the group message options.

You may customize the settings for your group talks in Google Messages.

Group conversations: Send an MMS response to all recipients.

Mass text: Send an SMS reply to all recipients and receive personalized responses.

Change how you send group communications.

- Open Google Messages.
- Tap your profile photo or icon, then select Messages Settings, Advanced, and Group Messaging.
- Choose bulk text or group MMS as your default.

How to join, exit, or rename a group conversation.

If all of your group members have RCS chats turned on, you can adjust the settings for group conversations:

- To add people to a group while in a discussion, touch More, then People & Options, and then Add People.

- To quit a group while in a conversation, tap More, then People & Options, and finally quit the group.

- When you create a group, you can name it. Only you can see the group's name.

- To rename a group, go to More > Group information. Tap the group's name and enter your new name. Tap OK.

GOOGLE MAIL

Instead of forwarding emails, use the Gmail app to read and send messages from Yahoo, Outlook, and other email accounts.

How to Add or delete an email account.

You can add both Gmail and non-Gmail accounts to the Gmail app on Android.

Add an account.

- launch the Gmail app.
- In the upper right corner, tap your profile picture.
- Tap "Add Another Account."
- Select the account type you want to add.
- Tap iCloud to sign in with your iCloud Mail, @me.com, or @mac.com account.

- If you use Outlook for Windows to check your work or school emails, choose Outlook, Hotmail, or Live.

- If you cannot find your email provider, select Other.

- To add your account, follow the on-screen instructions.

Remove an account.

- Launch Gmail on your device.

- Tap on your profile photo in the upper right corner.

- On this device, select Manage Accounts.

- Tap the email account you wish to remove.

- Choose Remove account.

- Switch or search all messages in your email accounts.

Switch email addresses.

- Launch Gmail on your device.

- Tap on your profile photo in the upper right corner.
- Tap the account you want to use.

Retrieve messages from all email accounts.

- Launch Gmail on your device.
- In the top left corner, hit Menu, and then All inboxes.

How to Sign in to Gmail.

To use Gmail, either sign in from a computer or add your account to the Gmail app for your phone or tablet. After you've logged in, navigate to your inbox to check your email.

Add your account.

The Gmail app for Android phones and tablets supports both Gmail and non-Gmail accounts.

- Open Gmail
- Tap the profile photo in the upper right corner.

- Tap "Add Another Account."
- Select the account type you want to add.
- To add your account, follow the on-screen instructions.

How to Change or reset your password.

You can change your password for security purposes or reset it if you forget it. Your Google Account password is required to access many Google products, including Gmail and YouTube.

Change your password!

- Open your device's Settings app and select Google, followed by Manage your Google Account.

- At the top, select Security.
- Under "How you sign in to Google," click Password. You might need to sign in.

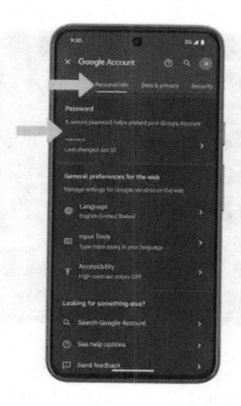

- Enter your new password and then press Change Password.

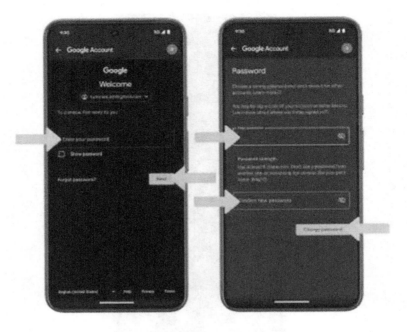

Tip: When typing your password on mobile, the initial letter is not case-sensitive.

Reset your password.

To retrieve your account, please follow the instructions outlined below. You will be given a few questions to authenticate your account, after which you will receive an email. If you don't get the email:

- Check your spam and bulk email folders.
- Add noreply@google.com to your contacts.

To request another email, complete the steps to regain your account.

1. Check all email addresses you may have used to sign up for or access your account.

2. Choose a password that you have not previously used for this account.

Sign-out options

The only way to sign out of the Gmail app is to delete your entire account from your phone or tablet.

However, many of the same tasks can be accomplished using other actions.

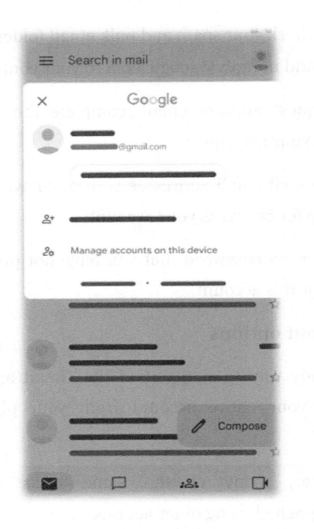

Delete your Google Account from your device.

When you delete an account, it is removed from all applications on the device. When you delete your account, you will no longer be able to access Google products such as Maps or YouTube.

This option is useful if you want to delete personal information from your device before giving it to someone else.

- launch the Gmail app.
- In the upper right corner, tap your profile picture.
- On this device, tap Manage Accounts.
- Choose an account.
- At the bottom, select Remove Account.

Tip: Removing the account from your phone does not delete the account itself, so you can continue to use it on a computer or other device.

Check emails from another account.

If you're using the latest version of the Gmail app, you'll only be able to check email from non-Gmail accounts. If these procedures do not work, please update the Gmail app and try again.

- Launch Gmail
- Tap on your profile photo in the upper right corner.
- Tap "Add Another Account."
- Select the account type you want to add.
- If you use Outlook for Windows to check your work or school emails, you can pick between Outlook, Hotmail, and Live.
- If you do not see your email service, select Other.
- To add your account, follow the instructions on the screen.
- Tap the account you want to use.

How to Create a Gmail account

To sign up for Gmail, you must first create a Google Account. Gmail, YouTube, Google Play, and Google Drive may all be accessed using the same username and password.

Register for a Gmail account.

- Go to the Google Account Sign-In page.

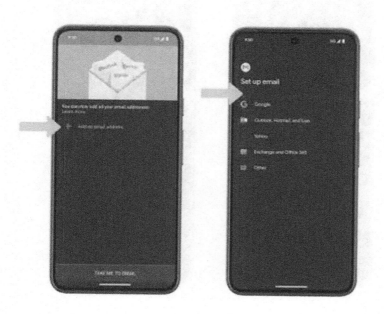

- Click "Create an account."

- To create your account, follow the on-screen prompts.

- To access Gmail, sign in using the account you created.

How to Read & organize emails

Add or remove inbox categories and tabs in Gmail.

Sort your emails into different inbox tabs, such as Social and Promotions. When you open Gmail, you do not have to see all of your emails at once.

Add or remove categories.

If you don't see categories like Primary or Social when you tap Menu, follow these steps to show them:

- launch the Gmail app.
- In the upper left corner, tap Menu
- Select Settings.
- Choose an account.
- Select Inbox type.
- Select the default inbox.
- Tap Inbox categories.

Move an email to a new category.

- Open an email.
- Tap Move To. If you don't see Move, tap More, then Move To.

- Tap a new category.

Make emails appear as primary.

Any emails marked with a star will appear in both your Primary and preceding categories.

- Launch Gmail
- Choose Star from your inbox or the email itself.

Check the number of emails in your inbox.

Gmail groups responses to messages into conversations. Your inbox will show the number of discussions but no messages.

Follow these procedures to find out how many messages are in your inbox.

- On your computer, open Gmail. The Gmail app does not show the total amount of messages you have.
- In the upper right corner, click Settings, then Settings.

- Scroll down to the "Conversation View" section.
- Turn the Conversation view off.
- At the bottom of the page, select Save Changes.
- Return to your inbox to check how many messages you have. If you have many sections or categories, please be sure to add the totals for each.
- When you're finished, return to settings and enable "Conversation view."

How to Report Spam in Gmail.

Gmail allows you to report unwanted emails as spam. Emails marked as spam are added to Spam. As you report more spam, Gmail improves its ability to identify similar emails as spam.

Report email as spam.

Important: When you report spam or move an email to Spam, Google receives a copy and may analyze it to protect users from spam and abuse.

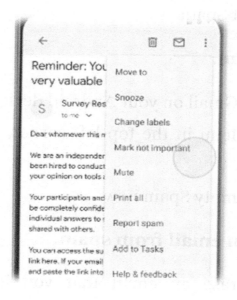

- Open Gmail on your Android device.
- Open the email that you wish to report as spam.
- Tap More in the top right corner, followed by Report Spam.

report multiple emails as spam.

- Tap the sender's profile picture next to each email in your inbox to report it as spam.
- Tap More in the top right corner, followed by Report Spam.

Delete spam.

- Open Gmail on your Android device.
- Tap Menu in the top left corner, followed by Spam.
- Tap Empty Spam now.

Remove an email from spam.

You can erase an email that you inadvertently tagged as spam.

- Open Gmail
- Tap Menu in the top left corner, followed by Spam.
- Open the email you want to delete.
- Tap More in the upper right corner, followed by Report Not Spam.

How to Delete and recover Gmail messages.

When you delete a message, it stays in your trash for 30 days. After 30 days, the message will be permanently erased from your account and unable to be restored.

Delete one or several messages.

- Launch Gmail on your Android device.

- To delete a message, tap the sender's profile image to the left of it.
- At the top, select Delete.

Delete several messages quickly

- Launch Gmail on your Android device.
- Tap the sender's profile photograph on the message's left side.
- In the upper left corner, tap the box next to "Select all."
- To choose more messages, scroll down and tap the box next to "Select all" again.
- At the top, select Delete.

Include "trash" as a swipe action.

Adding "Trash" as a swipe action allows you to rapidly archive messages in your inbox by swiping left or right.

- Launch Gmail on your Android device.

- Tap Menu in the upper left corner, then Settings, and finally General Settings.
- Tap Mail's swipe actions.
- Next to "Right swipe" or "Left swipe," select Change and then Trash.

Empty the trash

- On your Android device, launch the Gmail app.
- Tap Menu in the upper left corner, followed by Trash.
- At the top, select Empty Trash Now.

Recover messages from the trash.

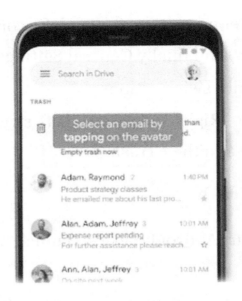

- On your Android device, launch the Gmail app.
- Tap Menu in the upper left corner, followed by Trash.
- Tap the sender's profile image to the left of each message to recover.
- Tap More in the top right corner, followed by Move To.
- In the "Move to" menu, select where you want to relocate the messages.

Search in Gmail.

You may find an email in your inbox containing search terms. Gmail proposes search terms as you type, allowing you to find what you're looking for faster. These search phrases are based on data from your Gmail account, such as messages, contacts, labels, and past searches.

How to Search.

- Launch Gmail on your Android device.
- Tap the Search Mail button at the top of the search window.
- Optional: Tap the Filter list, then choose a filter to narrow your results. Find out more about the available search filters.
- Enter your search criteria.
- Tap Search.
- Your results include all messages, excluding those marked as spam or trash.

- When you search for someone's email address, the results will include emails with their alias. To limit the search to only the original email, enclose the search in double-quotes. Example: "from:john.doe@gmail.com".
- When you search for "from email", the results will also include Drive files shared by that email address.

Clear the search history.

- On your Android device, launch the Gmail app.
- Tap the Menu button in the top left corner.
- Tap Settings, then General Settings.
- Tap the More icon in the upper right corner.
- Tap Clear search history, then Clear.

How to Send Google Drive attachments via Gmail.

When sending messages via Gmail, you can attach files from Google Drive, such as documents and photos. If the file exceeds the Gmail size limit or you want to work on it with others, attach it from Drive.

Send a Google Drive attachment.

- launch the Gmail app.
- Tap Compose.

- Tap Attach.

- Tap Insert from Drive.

- Tap the file you'd like to add.

- Tap Select.

- Tap Send.

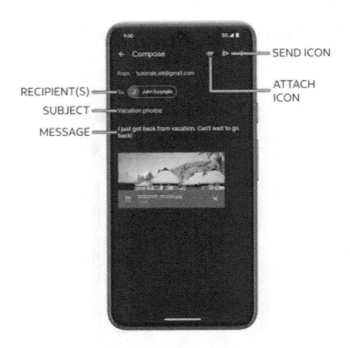

Sharing options for Google Drive files

When you attach a Google Drive file to a message, Gmail checks to verify if the recipients can access it.

If they don't, you'll be prompted to modify the file's sharing permissions before sending the message.

Share the link with anyone who has it.

- If you choose "Anyone with the link" as your sharing option, you may choose who can read, comment on, or change the file.
- If you forward the message or invite new participants to the chat, they will have the same permissions as the original recipients.
- To access or update the file, recipients do not need to have a Google account.

Share only with the email recipients.

If you only want your message's recipients to be able to view or edit the file, click "More options" when prompted to change your file settings.

If you keep the file private, recipients will be unable to view it.

Note: If a file cannot be shared with others, Gmail will warn you, and you may need to contact the file's original owner to change the sharing permissions.

How to Change your Gmail settings.

- Go to the Settings page.
- On your Android device, launch the Gmail app.
- In the upper left corner, tap Menu
- Tap General Settings or the account you wish to change.

How to Change your Gmail notifications.

You can customize how Gmail notifies you when you receive new emails. Your device determines which types of notifications you can customize.

Turn on or off Gmail notifications.

Step 1: Check your device's notification settings.

190

Important:

To receive Gmail notifications, turn on device notifications.

The settings change based on the phone

- Launch Gmail on your Android device.
- Tap Menu in the upper left corner, then Settings, and finally General Settings.
- Tap Manage Notifications.
- Turn all Gmail notifications on or off.
- You can also choose what types of notifications appear on your device.

Step 2: Check the Gmail app's notification settings.

Important: If you have multiple Gmail accounts, adjust the app notification settings for each one.

- Launch Gmail on your Android device.
- Tap Menu in the top left corner, then Settings.
- Select an account.

191

- Under "Notifications," click on Email notifications.
- Select the sorts of email notifications you want to receive.

All new emails: Receive notifications for every email you receive.

High priority only: Receive notifications for emails that Gmail has marked as high importance.

None: Disable any email notifications you get.

Tips:

- If you are still not receiving notifications, please check your sync settings:
- On the account settings page, scroll down to the "Data usage" section.
- Next to "Sync Gmail," check the box.

How to Change the Inbox Notification Settings.

- launch the Gmail app.

- Tap Menu in the top left corner, then Settings.
- Select an account.
- Under "Notifications," select Inbox notifications.
- Tap Sync Messages, then None, Last 30 Days, or All.
- Select your notification settings for your inbox.

Label the notifications: Receive notifications about new emails in your inbox.

Notify for all messages: Play a sound or vibrate when a new email arrives.

Change the label notification settings.

- launch the Gmail app.
- Tap Menu in the top left corner, then Settings.
- Select an account.
- Under "Notifications," select Manage labels.
- From the list, choose a label.

- Tap Sync Messages, followed by None, Last 30 Days, or All.
- Choose the notification settings for the label.

Label the notifications: Receive notifications for new emails in the label.

Notify of all messages: Make a sound or vibrate when a new email comes.

How to Change the notification sounds.

- On your Android device, launch the Gmail app.
- Tap Menu in the top left corner, followed by Settings.
- Select an account.
- Under "Notifications," select Notification Sounds.
- Under "Email" or "Chat and spaces," select Notification sound and then Sound.
- Select the notification sound you wish to use.
- To disable notification sounds, tap None.

HOW TO TAKE A PHOTO

You can take photos with your phone's camera in a variety of ways.

Take a photograph.

- Open the Google Camera application.

HOW TO TAKE A PHOTO

You can take photos with your phone's camera in a variety of ways.

Take a photograph.

- Open the Google Camera application.
- Point your camera and wait for it to focus.
- Tap Capture.

To zoom

Pinch open or close the screen, double-tap, or use the bottom slider.

Tip: When photographing from a distance, focus on your subject first to get the greatest detail.

Decide how to snap an image.

With your hands.

- Open the Google Camera application.
- Point your camera, then wait for it to focus and capture light.
- Tap Capture.

Using your voice.

respond with "OK Google, take a picture," or perhaps "OK Google, take a selfie."

Optional: Before shooting the photo, set the camera to wait 3 to 30 seconds. For example, "OK, Google, take a picture in 12 seconds."

Your Camera app will launch and take a photo.

How to Take selfies with your Pixel phone

You can use your Pixel device's front camera to capture a self-portrait

Flip your lens.

- Open the Google Camera application.
- To switch to the front camera, press Switch.
- Tap Capture.
- To take a selfie without using a button, simply twist your Phone away from you and back.
- To flip your lens again, repeat step 1.

Choose how your selfies are preserved.

You can save selfies as mirrored or unmirrored photos. If you save a selfie as a preview, it will not display inverted when you take a new selfie.

- To mirror or not mirror your selfies, head to the top of your camera and press the Down arrow, then Settings. Tap Save selfie as previewed.

Change the appearance of a selfie.

Retouch a selfie.

Face editing can be applied to selfies or images taken in portrait mode.

- To modify a selfie or portrait mode shot, use the Down arrow.
- Under "Face Retouching":
- Tap Subtle or Smooth.

Tip: The face editing results are only evident in the final image.

Brighten a selfie.

To brighten selfies, first use the front camera. To brighten selfies, tap the Down arrow, then Selfie Illumination.

Take a selfie using the timer.

- Open Google Camera.
- At the top, select Settings.
- On the "Timer" screen, select three or ten seconds.
- To start the timed countdown, tap Capture.

Set a selfie timer with your hand

Set a selfie timer with your hand on your Pixel

- Open the camera application.
- When your device's camera timer is enabled, raise your hand in front of the camera to start the countdown.
- To utilize the Palm Timer, make sure your face is in the frame.
- Your palm is straight and toward the camera.
- Both your face and palm are visible.

Take a selfie with your voice.

Google Assistant lets you shoot a hands-free photo with your voice on your Pixel device.

Take a hands-free photo using your voice:

- Open the camera application.
- Position your smartphone on a stable surface.
- Step away from the camera and into the picture.
- To start a camera timer with your voice, say "OK, Google, take a picture." After a three-second wait, your phone will take a snapshot.

Take low-light or night sight shots with your Pixel phone

When your device is steady, you can photograph low-light scenes like the night sky without needing a flash.

Use Night Sight to take low-light images.

- Open the Google Camera application.
- In the Photo mode carousel, choose Night Sight.
- Tap Capture.
- Hold steady for a few seconds as your device captures the photo.

To turn off Automatic Night Sight in Photo mode:

- On the right, select Night Sight.
- To make adjustments, move the slider from max to off.
- Select Settings.

- Set More Light to None.

Tips:

- When you capture a shot in low light using shot or Portrait mode, Night Sight is immediately active.
- When the camera flash is turned on, the Automatic Night Sight does not function.

To disable the More Light option

- launch the Camera app.
- Tap Settings in the lower left corner, then More Light.
- Turn off more lights.

How to capture images of the night sky.

You may take photos of the night sky with your Pixel. To do so, get away from the city lights. Take images of the stars between 45 and 90 minutes after sunset.

To take a photo:

- Go to a darker area.

- Open the Google Camera application.

- Tap Night Sight.

- Place your device on a stable surface, like a rock or a tripod. Don't use your hand.

- When your smartphone is still and ready, the shutter will switch to Astrophotography mode.

- Tap the shutter.

- Do not touch your cellphone until it has completed taking the photo. Your device will show a countdown timer.

Turn off automatic time-lapse:

- Open Google Camera.

- Tap Settings in the lower left corner, then More Settings and Advanced.

- Turn off the timelapse feature for astrophotography.

How to Record a video with your Pixel phone.

On your phone, you can record both in real-time and slow motion. You can also create time-lapse videos that speed up when played.

- To quickly record a video, launch the Camera app and then tap and hold Capture.
- Open the Google Camera application.
- If you are currently in photo mode, switch to video mode.
- To start recording, tap Record.

- To add a cut to your video, tap Pause. To resume recording, tap Record.

- Tap Capture to shoot a high-quality photo while recording video.

- Tap Stop to halt the recording.

How to Use Video Effects.

Make a video smoother

- Open the Google Camera app.
- If you are in photo mode, switch to video mode.
- Tap Video Settings in the bottom left corner, followed by Stabilization.
- Select the type of stabilization you prefer.
- Select Standard to capture light movement.
- To shoot still shots, tap Locked.
- Tap Active to record rapid movement.
- You can adjust the level of stability for each mode.

Get cinematic video effects

When you record in Cinematic mode, you can blur the background while keeping the subject in focus. To enable the cinematic mode:

- Open your phone's Google Camera app.

- If you're in camera mode, change to video mode.
- Swipe to activate Cinematic Blur mode.
- Tap the shutter to begin recording.
- Tap the subject to shift the focus.

Obtain rich video colors

When you capture video in HDR, the colors are bright. To activate 10-bit HDR video:

- Open the camera app
- If you are currently in photo mode, switch to video mode.
- Tap the Video Settings icon in the lower left corner.

Turn on high-resolution video.

- Open the camera app.
- If you're in camera mode, change to video mode.

- Tap the Video Settings icon in the lower left corner.
- Under "Resolution," choose 4K.
- Under "Frames/Sec," select 60fps.

Take a slow-motion video.

To create a slow-motion video:

- Open the Google Camera application.
- If you are currently in photo mode, switch to video mode.
- Switch to slow motion.
- To start recording, tap Record.
- Tap Capture to shoot a high-resolution photo while filming a slow-motion video.
- Tap Stop to halt the recording.

Tip: When recording exceptionally fast speeds in slow motion, use 1/8x.

How to Create a time-lapse video.

To document slow changes over time, such as a sunset:

- Open the camera app.
- If you are currently in photo mode, switch to video mode. Open the video mode, then select Time Lapse.
- To choose a faster time option, touch Auto in the bottom right corner.
- Select a speed choice. For example:
- Tap five times to convert 50 seconds in real time to 10 seconds in video.
- Tap 120 times to convert 20 minutes in reality to 10 seconds in the video.
- Tap the record button.
- Tap Capture to shoot a high-resolution photo while creating a time-lapse video.
- Tap Stop to halt the recording.

Tip: If you are unsure of the speed to use or how long to record, choose Auto.

Turn on Night Sight and Time Lapse:

- Open the camera app.

- If you are currently in photo mode, switch to video mode. Open the video mode, then select Time Lapse.

- Tap Settings in the lower left corner, then More Light.

- Tap Night Sight.

- Tap the record button. Keep your phone steady while it records the video.

- Tap Stop to halt the recording.

How to Delete, store, or locate an image or video on your Pixel phone.

Google Photographs on your Pixel phone lets you delete, store, and discover photographs and videos.

Delete all photographs and videos.

- On your Android device, open the Google Photos app.
- Sign into your Google account.
- Tap and hold the photo or video that you want to delete. You can select multiple items.
- At the top, pick Trash Delete.

Important:

- If you remove a backed-up photo or video from Google Photos, it will remain in your trash for 60 days.
- If you delete something from your Android device without backing it up, it will stay in your trash for 60 days.
- If you see a photo or video in Google Photos that you believe you had erased, it could have been saved on a portable memory card. To remove it, open your device's gallery app.

Download your photographs and videos.

- On your Android device, open the Google Photos app.
- Select a photo or video.
- Tap More and then Download.

Find your photographs and videos.

When you enable backup, your photos will be stored on photos.google.com.

To find your photos:

- Open the Google Photos application.
- Tap Photos.

How to Edit a photo or video using your Pixel phone

Your Pixel allows you to edit or change the appearance of a photo. You may also edit older photographs and photos from other devices in your Google Photographs library.

How to Change the image format to RAW + JPEG.

When you enable RAW/JPEG in your camera's settings, images are saved in both JPEG and RAW formats. The RAW icon at the top of your photos distinguishes RAW from JPEG images.

To support RAW and JPEG files:

- Open Google Camera.
- Tap Settings in the lower left corner, then More Settings.
- Select Advanced from the "General Options" menu.
- Turn on the RAW and JPEG controls.

Turn on RAW.

- In photo mode, press the Settings button in the bottom left corner.
- Turn on RAW + JPEG.

To locate, display, and modify a raw file:

- Open the Google Photos application.
- The "RAW" flag in the gallery grid indicates that the RAW + JPEG photo pairs were captured with the RAW option.
- Tap to see RAW.
- You can see the JPEG image, but you can also access the RAW image by tapping the second tile.
- To make changes to RAW photos, tap Edit.
- When you edit RAW files with your preferred editor, you can select a Default RAW Editor directly from Google Photos.

Tip: If you enable backup in Google Photographs, your RAW photographs will be automatically backed up.

How to use raw files:

- Take a photo using Night Sight or the usual mode.

- Get to your home screen.

- **Gesture Navigation**: Swipe up from the bottom of the screen.

- **Three or two-button navigation**: Tap Home.

- Open Google Photos.

- Tap Library in the lower right corner, then Raw.

How to Straighten, modify, or crop a photo.

Use gridlines to straighten pictures.

- Open Google Camera.
- Tap the Settings icon in the lower left corner.
- Tap More Settings and then Grid Type.
- Select the type of grid you want.

Adjust the photo ratio.

- Open Google Camera.
- Tap the Settings icon in the lower left corner.

- Select a ratio option.

Wide crop (16:9).

Full picture (4:3).

Crop a photo.

- Locate the photo you wish to alter within the Photos app.
- Tap Edit Photo, then Crop.

Adjust the color, light, or blur of a photograph.

- To edit a photo in the Photo app, first locate it.
- Tap Edit, then Tools.
- From here, you can adjust a photo's light, color, or blur.

Photo unblur

Photo Unblur helps you fix fuzzy photos.

- Open the Photos app.
- Select the photo you wish to alter.

- Tap Edit Photo, Tools, and finally Unblur.

Tip: Photo Unblur works on both fresh and old photos in your photo library.

Pop

- In the Google Photos app, select Edit Photo, Tools, and Pop.
- Then, tweak the scale slider.

Colours pop.

- In the Google Photos app, go to Edit Photo, then Colour Pop.
- Next, tweak the color pop slider.
- You may adjust the lighting in your images of individuals. Portrait lighting is provided for photographing small groups of individuals from the waist up.
- In the Google Photos app, select Edit Photo, Tools, and then Portrait Light.
- To brighten the image, select Add Light.

- Place the white ring where you want more light.

Adjust the brightness manually or automatically:

- To change the brightness, use the slider.
- To let your device control the illumination, pick Auto.
- To soften shadows, hit Balance Light.

Adjust the brightness or shadows.

Adjust the brightness. On the right, use the slider to reduce or raise Brightness.

Adjust shadows: On the right, use the slider to lower or raise the Shadows.

Take a straightforward image with framing suggestions.

When the two lines meet and the angle is zero, your phone will be straight.

- Open the Google Camera application.
- Hold your phone steady. In the center of the screen, two lines appear: yellow and white.
- To align the lines, turn your phone left to right and tilt it forward and backward.
- When you point your phone up or down at a subject, the "Up/Down" indicator shows.
- To align the "Up/Down" indicator and capture a straight photo, rotate your phone from left to right and tilt it forward and backward.

Take a high-resolution (50 MP) photo.

You may snap high-resolution 50 MP images and tweak other settings like color and exposure.

Turn on high resolution.

- Open the Google Camera application.
- Select Settings from the bottom left, then the Pro tab.
- Set the resolution to 50 megapixels.

How to Use the Portrait mode to capture a portrait photograph.

To capture portrait photos:

Open the Google Camera application.

In the photo mode carousel, choose Portrait and then Capture.

To create a blurred background for your photograph:

- Open the Google Photos application.
- Tap Photos.
- Tap Edit Photo, Tools, and Blur.
- Move the Blur slider.

Improve your facial photos (Face Retouching).

Face Retouching can be used to change skin texture, under-eye tone, and brightness.

Turn on face retouching.

- Open the Google Camera application.
- In the bottom menu, choose Portrait, then Settings, and lastly Face Retouching.
- Select an option.

Off

Subtle and silky.

Use the Ultrawide zoom to get a wider photo.

Ultrawide Zoom lets you photograph more individuals and their surroundings.

- Open the Google Camera application.
- Pinch the screen to zoom out.
- Use auto-focus to adjust the subject's sharpness.
- Point your camera at the topic you want to focus on.
- Tap the subject. A white circle appears and moves across the screen with the person.

- Tap Lock to fix your focus and exposure on a moving subject.

How to Take panorama pictures.

- Open the Google Camera application.
- In the photo mode carousel, choose Panorama.
- Tap Capture.
- Hold the lens steady while moving the camera horizontally. Ensure that the white frame is properly aligned.
- To create a vertical panorama, rotate your phone vertically. Then, move your camera up or down.
- When you're done taking your photograph, tap Stop Recording.

Take a 360-degree photosphere.

You may use your Pixel camera to produce a variety of 360-degree photo spheres, such as panoramas and fisheye images. To create a 360-degree photosphere:

- Open the Google Camera application.

- On the photo mode carousel, choose Photo Sphere, then Capture.

- Place the target circle above a white dot. The dot will turn blue before disappearing.

- Move the camera to the next white dot, keeping the lens steady.

- Repeat until there are no more white dots, and then touch Done.

To change your Photo Sphere type:

- Tap the Settings icon in the lower left corner.

- To shoot a 360-degree photo, choose the Panorama photosphere.

- To shoot a horizontal photo, hit Horizontal.

- To take a vertical photo, tap Vertical.

- Tap Wide-angle to take a photograph with a huge arc.

- To capture a fisheye photo, pick a Fisheye.

How to Take a close-up with a macro focus.

Macro Focus enables you to catch minute details in photographs and videos, such as flower petals or dew drops.

To use macro-focus:

- Open the Google Camera application.
- Bring your device closer to the subject.
- Tap the screen to bring it into focus.
- Take a snapshot or video of the Macro bloom as it appears.

Tips:

- Do not shadow your subject or block the light source.
- Tap to enable or disable macro focus.
- To focus on a certain feature of your subject, tap the screen in the appropriate spot.

Take a picture or video from afar.

Take images of subjects at a distance. On some Pixel devices, the latest generation of zoom lenses allows you to zoom up to 30x.

- Open the Google Camera application.
- Focus on your subject.
- **For fast adjustments**: Tap the 2x and 5x zoom buttons above the shutter.
- **For more precision**: Pinch the screen or swipe over the zoom buttons to access the zoom slider.
- Tap your subject to focus.
- Take your snapshot.

Use the Magic Eraser to eliminate or reduce distractions.

- Locate the photo you wish to alter within the Photos app.
- Tap Edit, then Tools, then Magic Eraser.

- Tap a suggestion. You can also use the circle or brush to remove any unnecessary distractions from the shot.
- Tap Camouflage, and then use the brush to blend things into the image.
- To complete, tap Done.

How to Use the Audio Magic Eraser to eliminate unwanted sounds.

To eliminate undesirable sounds from videos, utilize Audio Magic Eraser on your Pixel phone.

- Open the Google Photos application.
- Tap the video you wish to edit.
- At the bottom, choose Edit, Audio, then Audio Eraser.
- Select Auto if you want your phone to automatically adjust the audio.
- To manually tune the sounds, tap on one and drag the slider.

- Tap the Save Copy button in the lower right corner.

Take portrait-style photos.

- Open the Google Camera application.
- Tap Portrait and then Capture.
- To see the improved version, tap the photo in the lower right corner.

Tip:

After capturing a photo, select Edit Photo, Tools, then Blur. Next, adjust the Blur slider.

How to Use Best Take to Improve Group Photographs.

If someone blinks or looks away in your group shots, Best Take will merge similar photos to create a single image in which everyone looks their best. Choose your favorite facial expressions for everyone and create your own Best Take.

How to edit a photo using Best Take:

- Open the Google Photos application.

- Select a photo from a collection of comparable photos that include one or more people.

- At the bottom, choose Edit, Tools, and Best Take.

- Tap a face bubble to choose a different expression.

- When you've completed it, tap Done.

Use Magic Editor to reinvent your photos.

How to utilize the Magic Editor:

- Open the Google Photos app on your Pixel device.

- Tap on the photo you want to alter.

- Tap Edit then Magic Editor.

- To use the preset effects in Magic Editor:

- When you're in Magic Editor mode, choose Preset Edit Fix Auto.

- Select a preset.

- To navigate your options, swipe left.

- Tap the "Done" checkbox.
- If you wish to keep tweaking your photo, repeat steps 1-3.
- When you're finished editing, tap Save Copy.

How to Change the camera app's settings.

You can change your photo and video settings. For example, you can enable or disable location stamps, save storage space, and control dirty lens warnings.

How to Turn off the shutter sounds.

- Open the Google Camera application.
- Tap Settings in the lower left corner, then More Settings.
- Turn off the camera sound.

Disable photo and video location stamps.

- Open the Google Camera application.
- Tap Settings in the lower left corner, then More Settings.

- Turn off Save Location.

Tip: To view the timestamp for any photo, tap the photo in the bottom right corner and choose More. If you leave location stamps on, you will also get the photo location.

Reduce the resolution to economize on storage space.

Photos

- Open the Google Camera application.
- Tap the Settings icon in the lower left corner.
- Under "Photo," choose Full or Medium resolution.

Videos

- Open the Google Camera application.
- Switch to video mode.
- Tap the Settings icon in the lower left corner.
- Next to "Resolution," select Full HD.

How to Check the photo and video storage capacity.

To figure out how many photos and minutes of video you can record with your Pixel phone:

- Open the Google Camera application.
- Tap Settings in the lower left corner, then More Settings and Device Storage. The remaining storage space is displayed at the top of the screen.
- **To optimize storage space:** Turn on the storage saver.
- **To delete the files:** Tap Free Up Space.

Turn off the dirty lens alert.

If your camera detects a dirty lens, it may show a warning message. Turn off the following messages:

- Open the Google Camera application.
- Tap Settings in the lower left corner, then More Settings and Advanced.
- Disable the Show dirty lens warning.

Change what your volume buttons do.

- Open the Google Camera application.
- Tap Settings in the lower left corner, then More Settings.
- Tap Gestures and then Volume Key Action.
- Select an option.

How to Turn on the Flashlight.

Turn on the flash to take brighter photos:

- Open Google Camera.
- Tap Settings in the lower left corner, followed by Flash.

How to Scan documents using your Pixel phone

You may use your Pixel phone or tablet to digitize a physical document.

Scan a paper with your camera app.

- On your Pixel phone, open the Google Camera app.
- Point the device's camera to the document. Wait until the "Scan Document" prompt appears.
- Tap Scan Document.
- Follow the on-screen directions.
- To clean any area of the document, touch Clean at the bottom, then Apply.
- To save the document, press Done in the upper right corner, then choose Save, Download, or Share.

Scan a document with your Drive app.

On your Pixel phone or tablet, select the Google Drive icon.

- To scan a document, choose one of the following options at the bottom right:
- Tap Plus and then Scan
- Tap the camera.
- Point the device's camera to the document. Wait until the "Scan Document" prompt appears.
- Tap Scan Document.
- Follow the on-screen directions.
- To clean any area of the document, touch Clean at the bottom, then Apply.
- To save the document, press Done in the upper right corner, then choose Save, Download, or Share.

How to open and close the camera app on your Pixel phone.

Open the camera application.

You can open your camera in a variety of ways.

- Launch your phone's camera app.
- Double-press the power button on our phone.
- respond "OK, Google, take a picture." After a three-second wait, your phone will take a snapshot.

Close the Camera app.

- From the Camera app.
- Swipe up from the bottom, hold, then let go.
- Then, swipe up on the app.

TIPS AND TRICKS

Customize your home screen.

The Pixel 8a's default home screen configuration is simple.

- Long-tap the Pixel 8a home screen, then choose Wallpaper and Style.
- Change the background, set the Material You theme based on it, enable themed icons, and personalize app grids.

Use Circle to Search.

The Pixel 8a is loaded with AI capabilities. Circle to Search is a popular add-on that allows you to rapidly search for relevant information. You no longer need to switch between apps. Check it out in action by following the instructions below.

- Open a web page or app, then long-press the bottom menu bar.

- It triggers Circle to Search. Tap on an image, text, or video to find what you're searching for.
- Trigger circle for searching on Pixel 8a.
- Use the circle to search for Pixel 8a.
- The system initiates a Google search. Swipe up from the bottom to view the results.

Use Face Unlock to unlock applications.

The Tenson G3 and powerful machine learning algorithms allow you to use Pixel 8a Face Unlock for NFC transactions, banking, and app signing. Here's how to turn it on.

- Open Settings and go to Security & Privacy.
- Select Device Unlock.
- Tap Fingerprint and Face Unlock.
- Tap Face Unlock to register your face.
- Follow the on-screen directions.
- Turn on the "Verify it's you" option in apps.

Use focus mode.

Focus mode pauses distracting apps and hides their notifications. To activate and personalize it, follow the instructions below.

- Open Settings and select Digital Wellbeing and Parental Controls.
- Select Focus mode.
- Tap Turn on Now to personalize your list of distracting apps.

You may activate Bedtime mode from the same menu.

Use the Audio Magic Eraser.

Audio Magic Eraser eliminates annoying background sounds like wind, people, traffic noise, and more, resulting in clean, clear audio in a video. The capability is built within the Google Photos app and is compatible with any video.

- Open Google Photos and select a video.
- Tap Edit.
- Slide to Audio, then pick Audio Eraser.

- The technology recognizes different sorts of audio in a video.
- To eliminate noise, select an audio waveform and click the appropriate buttons.

Customize your Pixel 8a's lock screen.

Android 14 allows lock screen customization for the Pixel series. Here's how to customize your Pixel 8a with different clock styles and app activities.

- Open the Wallpaper and Style menu
- Select Lock Screen.
- Examine the various clock styles and sizes, and use the shortcuts in the lower corners.

Enable clear calling.

Clear Calling removes noise from active calls, enhancing the overall call quality for all participants. Go to Settings > Sound & Vibration > Clear Calling and turn on the toggle in the following menu.

Enable live translation.

Live Translate recognizes and shows translations for additional languages in the same app. You must activate it and download the appropriate languages for your Pixel 8a. Navigate to Settings > System > Live Translate and turn on the toggle. Tap Add a language to download additional Live Translate languages.

Add a language on Pixel 8a and customize Quick Tap settings.

Quick Tap is a commonly ignored feature of the Pixel UI. Double-tap the rear of your Pixel phone to snap a screenshot, launch a digital assistant, play/pause media, and other functions. On your Pixel 8a, click Settings and go to System > Gestures > Quick Tap to Start Actions. Turn on the gesture and choose a suitable action from the bottom menu.

Check to see if someone is tracking you.

The proliferation of Bluetooth trackers has raised questions about user privacy and safety. Google has a useful security function that detects a nearby unexpected tracker. The option is activated by default, but you can also initiate a scan manually.

Go to Settings > Security and Privacy > Device Finder > Unknown Tracker Alerts. Turn on the Allow Alerts toggle and do a manual scan from the same menu. You may now simply identify any strange stalkers traveling with you.

Made in the USA
Monee, IL
13 August 2024

63820991R00142